SIMPLY
THE BEST
★★★★★★★★★★★★★★★★★★★★
CALIFORNIA
★★★★★★★★★★★★★★★★★★★★
BARBECUE
RECIPES

CAROLYN HUMPHRIES

foulsham
LONDON • NEW YORK • TORONTO • SYDNEY

foulsham

The Publishing House, Bennetts Close,
Cippenham, Slough, Berkshire, SL1 5AP, England

ISBN 0-572-02508-4

Copyright © 1999 W. Foulsham & Co. Ltd.

Cover and text illustrations by Sophie Azimont

Printed in Great Britain by Cox & Wyman Ltd., Reading, Berks

CONTENTS

INTRODUCTION

In this book, I've tried to capture some of the true taste of California. People from different nationalities and cultures all over the world have settled there, bringing with them their own culinary influences; the fire of Mexico and Spain, the delicacy of Japan, the fragrant spices of Thailand and China, the colour and richness of the Mediterranean – all have found their way into Californian cooking. Added to this, the American West Coast offers an abundance of fresh fish, meat and poultry and exotic fruits and vegetables, which, together with a glorious climate, make barbecuing a way of life for the Californian people.

The recipes here have all been chosen to bring that authentic Californian style into your barbecue. Healthy, delicious and always elegant, they will make outdoor eating a real delight, with, I hope, a taste of sunshine.

Notes on the Recipes

* All ingredients are given in metric, imperial and American measures. Follow only one set in a recipe. American terms are given in brackets.
* All spoon measurements are level: 1 tsp = 5 ml;
  1 tbsp = 15 ml.
* Eggs are medium unless otherwise stated.
* Always wash, peel and core, if necessary, all fresh produce before use.
* Seasoning and the use of strongly flavoured ingredients such as garlic or chillies are very much a matter of personal taste. Adjust seasonings to suit your own palate.
* Always use fresh herbs unless dried are specifically called for. If you wish to substitute dried for fresh, use only half the quantity or less as they are very pungent. Frozen chopped varieties have a better flavour than the dried ones.
* Californians use a good-quality vegetable oil unless a particular type, such as olive oil, is called for. I prefer to use sunflower, but the choice is yours.
* I have given the choice of butter or sunflower spread in the recipes. Use a different margarine if you prefer but check that it is suitable for general cooking, not just for spreading.
* Use good-quality heavy-duty foil for barbecue cooking (some cheap kitchen foils are very thin).
* Make use of kitchen gadgets to speed up preparation: a food processor is wonderful for grating, slicing, kneading, beating or puréeing.
* Cooking times are approximate and will depend on personal preference as well as the heat of your barbecue and how far from the coals you set the rack. See the tips on page 13 on preparing the barbecue for cooking.

STORECUPBOARD STANDBYS

If you enjoy barbecues, take a leaf out of an organised Californian cook's book and keep a few basics in your storecupboard and freezer so that you can create great-tasting meals whenever the whim takes you.

In the Cupboard

* Spices like chilli powder and/or cayenne, cinnamon, cumin, coriander (cilantro), Chinese five spice powder, ginger, nutmeg.
* Dried herbs such as bay leaves, oregano, marjoram, rosemary, thyme and mixed herbs.
* Sauces like Tabasco, Worcestershire, tomato ketchup (catsup), soy sauce, tomato purée (paste), pesto sauce, mayonnaise. (I use a low-calorie French-style one.)
* Favourite relishes and pickles, including passata (sieved tomatoes).
* Seasonings like salt and freshly ground black pepper, ready-made mustards.
* Seeds and nuts like sesame, poppy and caraway seeds, pecans, peanuts, walnuts, hazelnuts (filberts) and almonds (keep just one or two types at a time as they can go rancid if not used).
* Vinegars such as red or white wine vinegar, balsamic and fruit vinegars.
* Lemon and lime juice, pure fruit juices.
* Olive oil, good-quality vegetable or sunflower oil.
* Garlic, onions and fresh root ginger.
* Clear honey, sugar, golden (light corn) syrup.

* Pasta and rice for accompaniments.
* Canned vegetables, pulses and vegetable mixtures like tomatoes, sweetcorn (corn), red kidney beans and ratatouille.
* Canned fruits.
* Canned fish such as anchovies, salmon, tuna.
* Crackers, melba toast, vacuum-packed part-baked speciality breads or rolls.

In the Freezer

* Large and small prawns (shrimp), other shellfish like scallops.
* Firm-fleshed fish like monkfish. Cut into cubes and freeze ready to make kebabs.
* Whole fish like trout or mackerel or a large fish like a salmon or sea bass when on special offer.
* Good-quality burgers, sausages and bacon.
* Minced (ground) lamb, steak or turkey for meatballs or burgers.
* Good-quality cuts for barbecuing like chicken or turkey breasts, lamb, beef or pork fillet, chops and steaks.
* Frozen chopped herbs.
* Ice cream to accompany desserts.

ALL ABOUT BARBECUES

Equipment and Tools

You can spend as little or as much as you like on a barbecue, from a cheap metal free-standing drum with a rack or a low, rectangular Hibachi to a large kettle barbecue with a lid or a state-of-the-art gas barbecue with temperature controls. You could also build a permanent brick one on a patio or terrace or simply buy a disposable foil one whenever you fancy an outdoor cook-up. Ironically, the two ends of the spectrum are, arguably, the most reliable and certainly the easiest to light. A gas barbecue speaks for itself while the disposable ones are virtually foolproof to light, and heat up much more quickly than a conventional barbecue.

If you have a gas barbecue, make sure you check the gas cylinder before you start – there is nothing worse than running out of fuel whilst you are cooking. For charcoal barbecues, most people prefer to use briquettes or compressed charcoal rather than lump charcoal as they burn more slowly and give off more heat.

For the Fire

To ensure your barbecue lights and is controlled you will need:

* Charcoal, firelighters, tapers and matches.
* Foil to line the barbecue (it makes it easier to clean afterwards).
* Tongs for spreading the glowing coals.
* Poker for flicking grey ash off the coals.

* A sprinkler or spray bottle of water to douse the flames when they flare up.
* A small shovel for adding extra coals and for removing the ash when the cooking is complete.
* Bellows – just in case the fire needs a bit of a boost.
* A bucket of sand to put out the fire, if necessary, after cooking (when you become an expert at judging the amount of coals you need, you will simply be able to spread out the last few glowing coals and let them die down naturally).
* A bucket of water – in case the fire gets out of control.
* A wire brush to scrub the barbecue rack while still warm after cooking.

For the Food and Cooking

* Prepare foods for marinating, salads, sauces and relishes well in advance.
* Don't put foods out by the barbecue until you are ready to cook.
* Keep salads and relishes cool until you are ready to serve.
* Have a set of long-handled tools for transferring food to and from the coals and for turning it during cooking.
* Use a long-handled basting brush to baste foods or coat with a marinade during cooking.
* Use a hinged, wire-meshed rack for cooking fish, burgers or other foods that may break up during cooking.
* Soak wooden kebab skewers for at least an hour before putting the food on, to prevent burning during cooking.
* Use heavy-duty foil, shiny side up, for wrapping up food or for laying delicate foods on during cooking.

* Wear heat-resistant gloves and a large apron.
* Have a trolley or small table near the barbecue to hold the uncooked food, any sauces for basting and garnishes for after cooking.
* If necessary, as food cooks, wrap it in foil and keep it warm, either at the side of the barbecue or on a warming rack, while cooking the remainder.

For Serving

* Ideally, have a table to eat at – it is much more civilised than struggling with a plate on your lap!
* Put up an awning or umbrella for shade.
* Use suitable crockery (I like to use wooden platters as they keep food warm longer and are virtually unbreakable) and cutlery, including salad servers or tongs and serving spoons.
* Have ready plenty of glasses, bottle and can-openers, a water jug and ice bucket (or a coolbox with icepacks to keep drinks cold).
* Lay your table attractively with a tablecloth and sturdy napkins.
* Set out any condiments you will need.

Safety Suggestions

Barbecues can be dangerous so always bear the following in mind:

* Make sure the barbecue is set on a level surface in the open air, avoiding any overhanging trees or shrubs.
* Once lit, never leave the fire unattended.
* Keep children well away from the barbecue once lit.
* Never move a lighted barbecue.
* Never touch any part of the barbecue once lit. Very hot charcoal looks white and powdery, not glowing red.

* Choose wooden-handled tools. Metal ones can get hot, plastic ones may melt.
* Douse flare-ups quickly, using a fine spray.
* Don't dispose of the ashes after cooking until completely cold.
* If you do get burned, hold under cold running water until it no longer stings. Cover with a dry, sterile dressing, if necessary, and seek medical attention if severe.

Lighting the Fire

* Before you begin, for courtesy, tell your neighbours you are having a barbecue. The smoke (and smells) can be quite penetrating.
* Start preparing the barbecue at least 45 minutes before you want to cook.
* Line the barbecue with heavy-duty foil for easier cleaning. Open the vents if your barbecue has them.
* Arrange a few pieces of broken firelighters on the foil.
* Top with a few pieces of wood chips or lump charcoal, then put a few briquettes on top.
* Light the firelighters with a taper.
* When the charcoal is burning steadily, using long-handled tongs, spread out the glowing charcoal and add more briquettes at the edges.
* The fire is ready for cooking when the coals are turning white and powdery, NOT when they are red-hot.
* The coals will retain their heat for quite some time, so don't go on adding more when you have nearly finished cooking.
* If you have a lot of charcoal left on the fire when you have finished, douse with sand and leave until completely cold. If there is just a little hot charcoal left, spread out as far as possible and leave until cold.

Barbecue Cooking

Here are a few tried-and-tested tips to help you enjoy your
barbecue cooking and get the best results.

* Once the fire is lit, it will take about 30 minutes until
  it is white-hot and ready for cooking.
* Oil the barbecue rack and set it about 10 cm/4 in
  above the coals.
* The fire is ready if you can hold your hand just above
  the rack for 2–3 seconds only.
* The centre of the fire will always be the hottest, so
  remember this when arranging the food over it. Foods
  that need quick searing, like steak, need to go over the
  hottest part. More delicate foods, like fruit and
  vegetables, can go nearer the edge. Allow plenty of
  space around each piece of food. It is better to cook in
  batches than to overcrowd the rack. Also, if there is too
  much food on at once, it is difficult to tend to it.
* Plan your cooking so you start with foods that take the
  longest time and add other foods as you go. Once they
  are well on the way to being cooked, they can be
  moved towards the edge of the barbecue and raw foods
  added to the centre.
* Remember to put any sauces or breads to warm at the
  edge of the barbecue while cooking the rest of the
  food.
* Cooked food can be kept hot in a roasting tin (pan),
  wrapped in foil, at the edge of the barbecue while you
  cook the remainder. If necessary, you can always put it
  back over the hot coals for a few seconds before
  serving.
* Always make sure food is thoroughly cooked through.
  To be on the safe side, part-cook foods such as chicken
  legs or ribs in your oven or on the hob before putting
  them on the barbecue to finish cooking.

Basic Cooking Times

Here's a guide to cooking simple barbecue fare, either marinated first or simply brushed with oil and seasoned before cooking. Of necessity, the times given are approximate as the time needed will depend on the size and shape of the food item and the heat of the fire.

A word of warning: avoid testing food repeatedly by piercing it with a fork or skewer. All the juices will run out and the results will be dry and disappointing.

Food	Size	Cooking time per side
Hamburger	2.5 cm/1 in thick	6 minutes
Beef steak	2.5 cm/1 in thick	5–8 minutes
Chicken/ turkey breast		8–10 minutes
Chicken portion with bone		15–20 minutes
Duck breast		10 minutes
Duck portion with bone		15–20 minutes
Fish, whole	large	10–12 minutes
	small	3–6 minutes
Fish steaks	2.5 cm/1 in thick	3–5 minutes
Fish fillets		2–4 minutes
Ham/gammon steaks	1 cm/½ in thick	5 minutes
Kebab poultry		4–5 minutes
meat		3–5 minutes
seafood		2–3 minutes
Lamb chop or steak	2 cm/¾ in thick	6–8 minutes
Pork chop or steak	2 cm/¾ in thick	10 minutes
Sausages	thin	4–5 minutes
	thick	6–8 minutes

APPETISERS

While your guests are sipping their first cocktail, cook
up some of these tasty morsels to get their taste buds
tingling. Appetisers should never be so big as to
completely satisfy the appetite, they should simply set
the scene for the main course to come.
All these dishes can be prepared in advance and take
only a few minutes to cook.

~~~~~~~~~~~~~~~~~

Chorizo with Churrasco Salsa

Serves 4

	METRIC	IMPERIAL	AMERICAN
Chorizo sausages	375 g	12 oz	12 oz
Salsa:			
Olive oil	60 ml	4 tbsp	4 tbsp
Sweet sherry	30 ml	2 tbsp	2 tbsp
White wine vinegar	20 ml	4 tsp	4 tsp
Lemon juice	5 ml	1 tsp	1 tsp
Shallot, very finely chopped	1	1	1
Garlic clove, crushed	1	1	1
Finely chopped parsley	30 ml	2 tbsp	2 tbsp
Chopped oregano	10 ml	2 tsp	2 tsp
A good pinch of chilli powder			
Salt and freshly ground black pepper			
Fresh crusty bread, to serve			

1 Brush the sausages with a little of the olive oil ready for barbecuing.

2 Whisk the remaining ingredients together well, cover and leave to allow the flavours to develop.

3 Barbecue the sausages for 2–3 minutes on each side until hot through and sizzling.

4 Cut into chunks, pour the salsa over and serve with lots of crusty bread to mop up the juices.

Calamares a la Parilla

Serves 4

	METRIC	IMPERIAL	AMERICAN
Baby squid, cleaned, reserving the tentacles	8	8	8
Garlic clove, crushed	1	1	1
Fresh breadcrumbs	60 ml	4 tbsp	4 tbsp
Chopped parsley	45 ml	3 tbsp	3 tbsp
Salt and freshly ground black pepper			
Lemon juice	5 ml	1 tsp	1 tsp
Finely grated lemon rind	5 ml	1 tsp	1 tsp
Olive oil	60 ml	4 tbsp	4 tbsp
Lemon wedges, to garnish			

1 Rinse the squid and pat dry on kitchen paper (paper towels).

2 Finely chop the tentacles and mix with the garlic, breadcrumbs, 30 ml/2 tbsp of the parsley, a little salt, lots of pepper, the lemon juice and rind. Moisten with 30 ml/2 tbsp of the olive oil.

3 Spoon this mixture into the squid and secure the ends with soaked wooden cocktail sticks (toothpicks).

4 Brush with more of the oil and barbecue for 6 minutes, turning once, until the squid is turning golden at the edges.

5 Remove the cocktail sticks and serve garnished with lemon wedges and the remaining chopped parsley sprinkled over.

Stuffed Chillies

Serves 4–8

	METRIC	IMPERIAL	AMERICAN
Large Californian or New Mexican chillies	16	16	16
Can of pinto or red kidney beans, rinsed and drained	200 g	7 oz	1 small
Button mushrooms, finely chopped	50 g	2 oz	2 oz
Small garlic clove, crushed	1	1	1
Ground cumin	2.5 ml	½ tsp	½ tsp
Dried oregano	2.5 ml	½ tsp	½ tsp
Tomato purée (paste)	10 ml	2 tsp	2 tsp
Frozen chopped spinach, thawed	100 g	4 oz	4 oz
Cheddar cheese, grated	50 g	2 oz	½ cup
Salt and freshly ground black pepper			
Olive oil	15 ml	1 tbsp	1 tbsp

1 Cut the stalk ends off the chillies and remove the seeds.

2 Mash the beans with a fork. Work in all the remaining ingredients except the oil.

3 Spoon the mixture into the chillies, pressing down well.

4 Brush with oil and wrap two or four stuffed chillies, side by side, in squares of oiled foil.

5 Cook over hot coals for about 20 minutes, turning occasionally, until the chillies are tender. Remove from the foil to serving plates and serve hot.

Warm Goats' Cheese with Fragrant Sun-dried Tomatoes

Serves 6

	METRIC	IMPERIAL	AMERICAN
Sun-dried tomatoes in oil, drained	6	6	6
Sun-dried tomato oil	30 ml	2 tbsp	2 tbsp
Finely chopped rosemary	15 ml	1 tbsp	1 tbsp
Finely chopped parsley	15 ml	1 tbsp	1 tbsp
Garlic clove, crushed	1	1	1
Freshly ground black pepper			
Cylinder-shaped goats' cheeses, 85 g/3½ oz each	2	2	2
Olive oil	15 ml	1 tbsp	1 tbsp
Slices of French stick	6	6	6

1 Finely chop the sun-dried tomatoes and mix with the tomato oil, rosemary, parsley, garlic and a good grinding of pepper. Cover and chill until ready to serve.

2 Cut each cheese into six slices. Brush with the olive oil.

3 Lay a sheet of heavy-duty foil on the barbecue, shiny side down. Lay the bread slices and the cheese on the foil and cook for about 2½ minutes, turning the bread halfway through cooking.

4 Transfer the bread to serving plates. Top with the cheese. Spoon the cold sun-dried tomato mixture on top and serve straight away.

Sizzling Avocado with Pecan Vinaigrette

Make sure your avocados are properly ripe or the result will be slightly bitter.

Serves 4

	METRIC	IMPERIAL	AMERICAN
Olive oil	45 ml	3 tbsp	3 tbsp
Walnut oil	15 ml	1 tbsp	1 tbsp
White wine vinegar	30 ml	2 tbsp	2 tbsp
Clear honey	10 ml	2 tsp	2 tsp
Finely chopped pecans	30 ml	2 tbsp	2 tbsp
A pinch of salt			
Freshly ground black pepper			
Ripe avocados	2	2	2

1 Whisk the oils, vinegar, honey, pecans, salt and pepper together in a small saucepan. Put on the side of the barbecue to warm.

2 Cut the avocados into halves, discarding the stones (pits).

3 Brush the cut sides with a little of the dressing, then lay, cut sides down, on the barbecue for 3 minutes. Turn over and cook, skin sides down, for a further 3 minutes.

4 Transfer to serving dishes and spoon in the warm dressing. Serve straight away.

Barbecued Oysters with Jalapeno Salsa

Serves 6

	METRIC	IMPERIAL	AMERICAN
Jalapeno chilli, seeded	1	1	1
Ripe tomatoes, skinned	3	3	3
Can of pimientos, drained	200 g	7 oz	1 small
Tomato purée (paste)	15 ml	1 tbsp	1 tbsp
Red wine vinegar	15 ml	1 tbsp	1 tbsp
Clear honey	5 ml	1 tsp	1 tsp
Salt and freshly ground black pepper			
Fresh oysters in their shells	18	18	18

1 Put the chilli in a blender or food processor with all the ingredients except the salt and pepper and the oysters.

2 Run the machine until fairly smooth. Season to taste. Turn into a small saucepan and warm at the side of the barbecue.

3 Open the oysters and remove the top shells. Add a good grinding of pepper to the oysters.

4 Carefully put the oysters in their shells on the barbecue rack and cook for about 3 minutes until the oysters sizzle. Lift on to serving plates. Spoon a little salsa over each and serve.

Tiger Prawns with Light Aioli

Serves 4

	METRIC	IMPERIAL	AMERICAN
Raw tiger prawns (jumbo shrimp), heads removed	24	24	24
Olive oil	30 ml	2 tbsp	2 tbsp
Lemon juice	15 ml	1 tbsp	1 tbsp
Large sprig of rosemary	1	1	1
Freshly ground black pepper			
Low-calorie mayonnaise	45 ml	3 tbsp	3 tbsp
Low-fat plain yoghurt	45 ml	3 tbsp	3 tbsp
Large garlic clove, crushed	1	1	1
Chopped parsley	15 ml	1 tbsp	1 tbsp
Lemon wedges and sprigs of rosemary, to garnish			

1   Lay the prawns in a shallow dish.

2   Whisk the oil and lemon juice together and pour over the prawns. Add the rosemary and a good grinding of pepper. Cover and chill for 2–3 hours, turning once.

3   To make the aioli, mix the mayonnaise with the yoghurt, garlic, parsley and plenty of pepper. Turn into a small bowl, cover and chill until ready to serve.

4   Thread the prawns on four soaked wooden skewers. Barbecue for about 4 minutes, turning occasionally and brushing with any remaining marinade.

5   Transfer to plates, garnish with lemon wedges and sprigs of rosemary and serve with the aioli.

Mammoth Mushrooms

Serves 4

	METRIC	IMPERIAL	AMERICAN
Large open mushrooms	4	4	4
Extra-lean pork sausagemeat	225 g	8 oz	8 oz
Low-fat soft cheese	100 g	4 oz	½ cup
Small red chilli, seeded and chopped	1	1	1
Chopped parsley	30 ml	2 tbsp	2 tbsp
Freshly ground black pepper			
Oil for brushing			

1 Peel the mushrooms. Remove the stalks and chop finely.

2 Dry-fry the sausagemeat with the mushroom stalks in a saucepan on the hob, for about 3 minutes, stirring, until cooked through and crumbly.

3 Remove from the heat and work in the cheese, chilli, parsley and some pepper.

4 Brush the mushrooms with oil. Spoon the sausage mixture into the caps.

5 Place on the barbecue rack and cook for about 10 minutes until tender and sizzling.

Refried Beans with Barbecued Chips

Serves 4

	METRIC	IMPERIAL	AMERICAN
Can of pinto or red kidney beans, rinsed and drained	425 g	15 oz	1 large
Dried oregano	2.5 ml	½ tsp	½ tsp
Hot chilli powder	2.5 ml	½ tsp	½ tsp
Salt and freshly ground black pepper			
Large green plantains	2	2	2
OR green bananas	3	3	3
Soya or sunflower oil	60 ml	4 tbsp	4 tbsp
Ground cumin	5 ml	1 tsp	1 tsp
Cheddar cheese, grated	50 g	2 oz	½ cup

1 Mash the beans with a potato masher and stir in the oregano and chilli powder. Season to taste.

2 Use a sharp pointed knife to cut the skin of the plantains, then peel it off. If using bananas, peel them. Cut into thin diagonal slices and place in a bowl.

3 Add 15 ml/1 tbsp of the oil and the cumin and toss well so that each piece is coated.

4 Arrange as many of the plantain or banana slices as will fit on a hinged wire rack. Cook for about 8 minutes on each side until golden, brushing with a little more oil during cooking. Transfer to a roasting tin (pan) at the side of the barbecue to keep warm and cook the remaining slices.

5 While the second batch is cooking, heat 15 ml/1 tbsp of oil in a saucepan over the coals. Add the mashed beans and cook, stirring, for about 3 minutes until thick and piping hot. Stir in the cheese.

6 Sprinkle the plantain or banana chips with salt. Spoon the beans into a small bowl and surround with the chips to dip in.

Devils on Horseback

Serves 4–6

	METRIC	IMPERIAL	AMERICAN
Ready-to-eat prunes, stoned (pitted)	24	24	24
Whole blanched almonds	24	24	24
Rashers (slices) of streaky bacon, rinded	12	12	12

1 Gently open the slit in the side of each prune and push an almond inside.

2 Cut each piece of bacon in half widthways and stretch with the back of a knife.

3 Roll up a stuffed prune in each piece of bacon and secure with a soaked wooden cocktail stick (toothpick).

4 Cook on foil on the barbecue for 3–4 minutes, turning once or twice, until golden and sizzling. Serve straight away.

Cheese and Olive Morsels

Serves 6–8

	METRIC	IMPERIAL	AMERICAN
Cheddar cheese, grated	100 g	4 oz	1 cup
Butter or sunflower spread	50 g	2 oz	¼ cup
Cayenne	1.5 ml	¼ tsp	¼ tsp
Made English mustard	1.5 ml	¼ tsp	¼ tsp
Plain (all-purpose) flour	75 g	3 oz	¾ cup
Stuffed green olives	36	36	36

1 Mash the cheese and butter or sunflower spread together.

2 Using a wooden spoon and then your hands, work in the cayenne, mustard and flour to form a firm dough.

3 Divide the dough into 36 pieces. Flatten each piece, place an olive in the centre and draw the dough up around the olive to enclose completely. Chill until ready to cook.

4 Thread on six soaked skewers and grill (broil) over moderate coals for about 12 minutes, turning frequently, until golden. Remove the skewers and serve in a bowl.

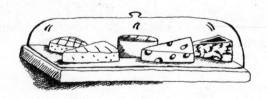

Nectarine and Serrano Ham Crostini

Serves 4

	METRIC	IMPERIAL	AMERICAN
Nectarines, skinned, halved and stoned (pitted)	2	2	2
Slices of ciabatta bread	8	8	8
Olive oil	30 ml	2 tbsp	2 tbsp
Wafer-thin slices of serrano ham, halved widthways	4	4	4
Bel Paese, Port Salut or other semi-soft cheese, rinded, if necessary, and sliced	175 g	6 oz	6 oz
Lollo rosso leaves, to garnish			
Light French Dressing (see page 126)			

1 Cut each nectarine half into four slices. Barbecue for 4 minutes, turning once, until turning slightly golden. Remove and keep warm at the side of the barbecue.

2 Drizzle the slices of bread with the olive oil. Place on the barbecue and cook until toasted underneath. Turn over and top each with a slice of serrano ham, then the cheese. Top each with two slices of nectarine and cook until the bread is toasted and the cheese is beginning to melt.

3 Transfer to serving plates and add a garnish of lollo rosso leaves with a little Light French Dressing spooned over.

Barbecued Buffalo Wings

Serves 6

	METRIC	IMPERIAL	AMERICAN
Shallots, finely chopped	2	2	2
Large garlic clove, crushed	1	1	1
Sunflower oil	45 ml	3 tbsp	3 tbsp
Clear honey	15 ml	1 tbsp	1 tbsp
Made English mustard	10 ml	2 tsp	2 tsp
Tomato ketchup (catsup)	120 ml	4 fl oz	½ cup
Tomato purée (paste)	90 ml	6 tbsp	6 tbsp
Red wine vinegar	90 ml	6 tbsp	6 tbsp
Worcestershire sauce	15 ml	1 tbsp	1 tbsp
Light soy sauce	15 ml	1 tbsp	1 tbsp
A few drops of Tabasco sauce			
Chicken wings	24	24	24
Guacamole Relish (see page 134), to serve			

1 Fry (sauté) the shallots and garlic in the oil for
2 minutes, stirring. Blend in all the remaining
ingredients except the chicken wings.

2 Cut the wing tips off the chicken wings at the first
joint and discard.

3 Add the chicken wings to the marinade and leave in a
cool place for at least 1 hour.

4 Thread the chicken wings on six long metal skewers.
Barbecue over hot coals for about 20 minutes, turning
occasionally and brushing with any remaining
marinade.

5 Serve hot with Guacamole Relish.

MEAT AND POULTRY

If you think a meat barbecue consists of sausages, burgers or great slabs of plain steak, think again. The Californian way uses a whole range of tender cuts of meat, flavoured with subtle herbs, spices, wines, fruits and sauces.

~~~~~~~~~~~~~~

Rosemary Chicken with Wine-caramelised Onions

Serves 4

	METRIC	IMPERIAL	AMERICAN
Small onions, peeled and halved	8	8	8
Chicken portions	4	4	4
Chopped rosemary	5 ml	1 tsp	1 tsp
Salt and freshly ground black pepper			
Red wine	120 ml	4 fl oz	½ cup
Light brown sugar	30 ml	2 tbsp	2 tbsp
Spiced Potato Skins (see page 94) and a green salad, to serve			

1 Cook the onion halves in boiling water for 3 minutes. Drain.

2 Put the chicken portions in a shallow pan. Sprinkle with the rosemary, salt and pepper. Arrange the onion halves around and pour the wine over. Cover and leave to marinate for at least 2 hours, turning occasionally.

3 Lift the chicken out of the marinade and pat dry on kitchen paper (paper towels).

4 Transfer the onions to a large sheet of foil, shiny side up. Add 90 ml/6 tbsp of the wine marinade and sprinkle with the sugar. Wrap up firmly.

5 Put the onion parcel on the barbecue and cook for 10 minutes. Turn the parcel over. Add the chicken to the barbecue and cook with the onions for about 30 minutes, turning the chicken occasionally and brushing with the remaining marinade until the chicken is tender and cooked through and the onions are richly caramelised.

6 Serve with Spiced Potato Skins and a green salad.

Spatchcock Poussins with Pesto

Serves 2 or 4

	METRIC	IMPERIAL	AMERICAN
Poussins (Cornish hens)	2	2	2
Pesto (from a jar)	60 ml	4 tbsp	4 tbsp
Olive oil	30 ml	2 tbsp	2 tbsp
Freshly ground black pepper			
Clear honey	30 ml	2 tbsp	2 tbsp
Focaccia with olives and Rocket, Grapefruit and Walnut Salad (see page 101), to serve			

1 To spatchcock each poussin, cut along both sides of the backbone from the parson's nose to the neck. Remove the backbone. Turn the bird over, press on the breastbone to flatten out and fold the drumsticks towards the centre. Push one soaked wooden skewer through one drumstick and out the other one and a second one through the wings.

2 From the neck end, ease the skin away from the breast. Spoon half the pesto under the skin. Brush all over with some of the oil and sprinkle with pepper.

3 Lay foil on the barbecue and brush with oil. Cook the poussins, skin-sides down, on the foil for 8 minutes. Turn over and brush the skin with the honey. Barbecue for about 20 minutes until cooked.

4 Transfer to serving plates and remove the skewers. Spoon over any juices. Serve with focaccia with olives and a Rocket, Grapefruit and Walnut Salad.

MacArthur Park Chicken

Serves 6

	METRIC	IMPERIAL	AMERICAN
Boneless chicken thighs, skinned	12	12	12
Garlic purée (paste)	5 ml	1 tsp	1 tsp
Tomato purée	15 ml	1 tbsp	1 tbsp
Freshly ground black pepper			
Emmental (Swiss) cheese, cut into 12 cubes	100 g	4 oz	4 oz
Rashers (slices) of extra-lean streaky bacon, rinded	12	12	12
Sunflower oil	30 ml	2 tbsp	2 tbsp
Lemon Glazed Potatoes (see page 90) and a green salad, to serve			

1   Open out the thighs on a board. Spread each with a very little of the garlic, then the tomato purée. Add a good grinding of pepper.

2   Put a piece of cheese in the centre of each and re-shape.

3   Stretch the rashers slightly by scraping gently with the back of a knife. Wrap one rasher round each thigh to cover completely. Secure with soaked wooden cocktail sticks (toothpicks).

4   Barbecue for about 25 minutes, turning frequently, until cooked through and the bacon is crisp and brown.

5   Serve with Lemon Glazed Potatoes and a green salad.

Thai Coconut Chicken

Serves 4

	METRIC	IMPERIAL	AMERICAN
Creamed coconut	50 g	2 oz	2 oz
Garlic clove, crushed	1	1	1
Small green chilli, seeded and chopped	1	1	1
Chopped coriander (cilantro)	15 ml	1 tbsp	1 tbsp
Shallot, finely chopped	1	1	1
Grated fresh root ginger	5 ml	1 tsp	1 tsp
Finely grated rind and juice of 1 small lime			
Chicken breasts, part-boned, with the skin on	4	4	4
Sunflower oil	75 ml	5 tbsp	5 tbsp
Freshly ground black pepper			
Thai Fragrant Rice Moulds (see page 108) and Warm Carrot and Mustard Salad (see page 109), to serve			

1   Heat the coconut gently in a small saucepan until melted. Stir in the the garlic, chilli, coriander, shallot, ginger and lime rind. Turn into a bowl and leave until cool and the mixture forms a thick paste.

2   Gently pull back the skin from the chicken breasts to form pockets. With your fingers, smear the coconut mixture between the flesh and the skin. Secure with wooden cocktail sticks (toothpicks).

3   Whisk the lime juice with the oil and a good grinding of black pepper. Brush all over the chicken.

4   Barbecue for 30 minutes, brushing with the oil and lime juice and turning once or twice during cooking.

5 Remove the cocktail sticks and serve with Thai Fragrant Rice Moulds and Warm Carrot and Mustard Salad.

Grilled Chicken Strips in Cantaloupes

Serves 4

	METRIC	IMPERIAL	AMERICAN
Olive oil	15 ml	1 tbsp	1 tbsp
Chicken stir-fry meat	350 g	12 oz	12 oz
Yellow (bell) pepper, diced	1	1	1
Bunch of spring onions (scallions), chopped	1	1	1
Light soy sauce	30 ml	2 tbsp	2 tbsp
Medium sherry	15 ml	1 tbsp	1 tbsp
A good pinch of ground ginger			
Salt and freshly ground black pepper			
Ripe cantaloupe melons, halved and seeds removed	2	2	2
Lettuce leaves, to garnish			

1 Heat the oil in a frying pan (skillet) over the coals.

2 Add the chicken, pepper and spring onions and stir-fry for 5–7 minutes until the chicken is tender.

3 Add the soy sauce, sherry and ginger. Toss well and season to taste.

4 Put the melons on serving dishes on a bed of lettuce leaves. Spoon in the chicken mixture and serve.

Chicken and Roast Vegetable Fajitas

Serves 4

	METRIC	IMPERIAL	AMERICAN
Large chicken breasts	4	4	4
Large garlic clove, crushed	1	1	1
Finely grated rind and juice of 1 lime			
Red chilli, seeded and finely chopped	1	1	1
Paprika	15 ml	1 tbsp	1 tbsp
Dried oregano	5 ml	1 tsp	1 tsp
Ground cumin	2.5 ml	½ tsp	½ tsp
Ground cinnamon	1.5 ml	¼ tsp	¼ tsp
Sunflower or soya oil	60 ml	4 tbsp	4 tbsp
Salt and freshly ground black pepper			
Red (bell) pepper, cut into 8 thick strips	1	1	1
Green pepper, cut into 8 thick strips	1	1	1
Aubergine (eggplant), sliced	1	1	1
Courgette (zucchini), cut into diagonal slices	1	1	1
Flour tortillas	12–16	12–16	12–16
A little tomato or chilli relish			
Low-fat crème fraîche	150 ml	¼ pt	⅔ cup
Onion, finely chopped	1	1	1
Iceberg lettuce, finely shredded	½	½	½

1 Wipe the chicken breasts and slash in several places with a sharp knife. Place in a shallow dish.

2 Mix together the garlic, lime, chilli, paprika, oregano, cumin and cinnamon with 30 ml/2 tbsp of the oil. Season lightly with salt and pepper and pour over the chicken. Turn to coat completely. Cover and leave to marinate for at least 1 hour.

3 Lay the peppers, aubergine and courgette on a large sheet of foil, shiny side up. Drizzle with the rest of the oil and season with salt and pepper. Wrap up the parcel and twist the edges together to seal. Barbecue for 25 minutes until the vegetables are just tender.

4 Wrap the tortillas in foil and warm at the side of the barbecue.

5 When the vegetables have been cooking for 10 minutes, add the chicken breasts and cook for 10–15 minutes, turning occasionally, until tender and cooked through.

6 Carve the chicken breasts into thin slices and place on large serving plates with the roasted vegetables and the flour tortillas.

7 To serve, spread the tortillas with a little relish, add the vegetables and chicken, top with a little crème fraîche, chopped onion and shredded lettuce, roll up and eat with the fingers.

Chicken Liver and Sage Brochettes with Persimmons

Serves 4

	METRIC	IMPERIAL	AMERICAN
Chicken livers, trimmed	450 g	1 lb	1 lb
Onion, quartered and separated into layers	1	1	1
A small handful of sage leaves			
Butter or sunflower spread, melted	75 g	3 oz	⅓ cup
Salt and freshly ground black pepper			
Orange persimmons	2	2	2
Long diagonal slices of French bread	4	4	4
Watercress, to garnish			
Tomato and Onion Salad (see page 103) and French Bean Salad (see page 104), to serve			

1 Rinse the chicken livers and pat dry on kitchen paper (paper towels).

2 Thread the chicken livers on soaked wooden skewers, interspersed with the onion pieces and sage leaves.

3 Brush all over with melted butter or spread and season with salt and pepper.

4 Cut the tops and bases off the persimmons and then cut into slices.

5 Brush a sheet of foil with a little of the remaining butter or spread. Arrange the persimmon slices on the foil in a single layer and brush again. Brush the slices of bread with the remaining butter or spread.

6 Place everything on the barbecue and cook, turning once, so that the bread is toasted on both sides, the chicken livers are just cooked but not hard and the persimmons are turning golden round the edges. Remove the bread once toasted and keep warm at the side of the barbecue.

7 Lay the toasted bread slices on serving plates. Top with the chicken liver brochettes and place the persimmon slices to one side. Garnish with watercress and serve with a Tomato and Onion Salad and a French Bean Salad.

Lamb Shanks with Mushroom and Garlic Potatoes

Serves 4

	METRIC	IMPERIAL	AMERICAN
Lamb shanks, about 200 g/7 oz each 4	4		4
Salt and freshly ground black pepper			
White wine vinegar	15 ml	1 tbsp	1 tbsp
Baby roasting potatoes, scrubbed	450 g	1 lb	1 lb
Button mushrooms	225 g	8 oz	8 oz
Olive oil	90 ml	6 tbsp	6 tbsp
Garlic cloves, crushed	2	2	2
Dried oregano	5 ml	1 tsp	1 tsp
Dried basil	5 ml	1 tsp	1 tsp
White wine	90 ml	6 tbsp	6 tbsp
Tomato and Onion Salad (see page 103), to serve			

1 Put the lamb in a large saucepan. Add a sprinkling of salt and pepper and cover with water. Add the vinegar. Cover, bring to the boil, reduce the heat and simmer gently for 1 hour. Drain.

2 Meanwhile, par-boil the potatoes in boiling, salted water for 6 minutes. Drain. Lay on a large sheet of foil, shiny side up, with the mushrooms. Drizzle with half of the oil. Add one of the crushed garlic cloves and season with salt and pepper. Wrap up securely.

3 Whisk the remaining ingredients together. Lay the lamb in a shallow dish and pour the baste over. Turn to coat completely. Season with salt and pepper.

4 Put the potatoes and the lamb on the barbecue and cook for about 30 minutes, turning and brushing the lamb with the baste until browned and tender. Turn the potato parcel once, halfway through cooking. Serve hot with a Tomato and Onion Salad.

Teryaki Kebabs

Serves 4

	METRIC	IMPERIAL	AMERICAN
Light soy sauce	30 ml	2 tbsp	2 tbsp
Medium sherry	30 ml	2 tbsp	2 tbsp
Garlic clove, crushed	1	1	1
A good pinch of ground ginger			
Clear honey	10 ml	2 tsp	2 tsp
Chicken breast, cut into cubes	350 g	12 oz	12 oz
Japanese Salad (see page 102), to serve			

1 Mix the soy sauce with the sherry, garlic, ginger and honey.

2 Add the diced chicken and toss well. Leave in a cool place to marinate for at least 2 hours.

3 Thread on soaked wooden skewers. Barbecue over hot coals for about 8–10 minutes, turning and brushing occasionally with any remaining marinade, until tender and cooked through.

4 Serve hot with an Japanese Salad.

Pork Tenderloin Brochettes with Kumquats

These are also delicious made with diced duck breasts.

Serves 4

	METRIC	IMPERIAL	AMERICAN
Medium sherry	60 ml	4 tbsp	4 tbsp
Light soy sauce	60 ml	4 tbsp	4 tbsp
Clear honey	45 ml	3 tbsp	3 tbsp
Grated fresh root ginger	5 ml	1 tsp	1 tsp
Chicken stock, made with ½ stock cube	100 ml	3½ fl oz	6½ tbsp
Kumquats	100 g	4 oz	4 oz
Pork tenderloin, cut into 16 cubes	350 g	12 oz	12 oz
Green (bell) pepper, cut into large dice	1	1	1
Red pepper, cut into large dice	1	1	1
Jacket Potatoes (see page 93), to serve			

1 Put the sherry, soy sauce, honey, ginger, stock and kumquats in a saucepan and bring to the boil. Cook for 2 minutes, then remove from the heat and cool.

2 Put the pork cubes in a shallow dish. Pour over the marinade, turn to coat completely, then cover and chill for several hours or overnight.

3 Thread the pork cubes on skewers with the kumquats and peppers.

4   Cook over hot coals, turning frequently and basting
with the marinade, for about 10 minutes or until
cooked through. Serve with Jacket Potatoes.

Peach Spare Ribs

Serves 6

	METRIC	IMPERIAL	AMERICAN
Short Chinese pork spare ribs	1.75 kg	4 lb	4 lb
Can of peach slices in natural juice, drained, reserving the juice	410 g	14½ oz	1 large
Cider vinegar	60 ml	4 tbsp	4 tbsp
Light soy sauce	45 ml	3 tbsp	3 tbsp
Garlic cloves, crushed	2	2	2
Grated fresh root ginger	5 ml	1 tsp	1 tsp
Tomato purée (paste)	15 ml	1 tbsp	1 tbsp

1   Trim any fat from the ribs and place them in a large
saucepan. Cover with water, bring to the boil, reduce
the heat and simmer gently for 1 hour. Drain and
place in a shallow dish.

2   Purée the peach slices in a blender or food processor
and mix with the vinegar, soy sauce, garlic, ginger and
tomato purée. Thin, if necessary, with a little of the
juice. Spoon over the ribs. Leave to marinade for
several hours or overnight, turning once or twice.

3   Drain thoroughly and barbecue over hot coals,
basting occasionally with any remaining marinade,
for about 30 minutes until the ribs are a rich brown
and meltingly tender.

Carpet Bag Steaks

Serves 4

	METRIC	IMPERIAL	AMERICAN
Fillet or thick rump steaks	4	4	4
Oysters	8	8	8
Butter or sunflower spread	15 g	½ oz	1 tbsp
Snipped chives	15 ml	1 tbsp	1 tbsp
A few drops of Tabasco sauce			
Salt and freshly ground black pepper			
Rashers (slices) of streaky bacon, rinded	4	4	4
A little oil for brushing			
Spinach, Cucumber and Kiwi Salad (see page 114), to serve			

1 Make a deep slit in the side of each steak to form a pocket.

2 Open the oysters, tip into a pan with their liquid, the butter or spread, chives, Tabasco and a little salt and pepper and fry (sauté) until the edges begin to curl.

3 Lift the oysters out of the pan. Boil the cooking juices until very well reduced and pour over the oysters. Toss and leave to cool.

4 Push two oysters inside each steak and add a little of the juices to each.

5 Stretch each bacon rasher with the back of a knife. Wrap one round each steak. Secure with a cocktail stick (toothpick), if necessary.

6   Cook over hot coals for 8–16 minutes, turning
    frequently and brushing with a little oil, until cooked.
    Serve with a Spinach, Cucumber and Kiwi Salad.

Chilli Meatballs

Serves 4

	METRIC	IMPERIAL	AMERICAN
Extra-lean minced (ground) lamb	350 g	12 oz	12 oz
Dried onion granules	10 ml	2 tsp	2 tsp
Chilli powder	2.5 ml	½ tsp	½ tsp
Ground cumin	5 ml	1 tsp	1 tsp
Finely chopped coriander (cilantro)	15 ml	1 tbsp	1 tbsp
Salt and freshly ground black pepper			
Sunflower oil	15 ml	1 tbsp	1 tbsp
Tomato ketchup (catsup)	15 ml	1 tbsp	1 tbsp
White wine vinegar	10 ml	2 tsp	2 tsp
Clear honey	5 ml	1 tsp	1 tsp
Conchiglie Mexicano (see page 105), to serve			

1   Mix the lamb with the onion, chilli powder, cumin
    and coriander. Season with salt and pepper.

2   Shape into 16 small balls. Thread on four soaked
    wooden skewers, squeezing the meat firmly round the
    skewers.

3   Whisk the remaining ingredients together. Barbecue
    the meatballs for about 12 minutes, basting liberally
    with this mixture and turning occasionally until
    cooked through and golden.

4   Serve with Conchiglie Mexicano.

Surf 'n' Turf with Capers and Mustard Mayo

Serves 4

	METRIC	IMPERIAL	AMERICAN
Fillet steaks, about 150 g/5 oz each	4	4	4
Sunflower oil for brushing			
Steak seasoning	15 ml	1 tbsp	1 tbsp
Raw king prawns (jumbo shrimp), shelled but tails left on	12	12	12
Juice of ½ lemon			
Low-calorie mayonnaise	90 ml	6 tbsp	6 tbsp
Crème fraîche	45 ml	3 tbsp	3 tbsp
Dijon mustard	5 ml	1 tsp	1 tsp
Capers, chopped	15 ml	1 tbsp	1 tbsp
Vinegar from the capers	15 ml	1 tbsp	1 tbsp
Chopped parsley	15 ml	1 tbsp	1 tbsp
Freshly ground black pepper			
Sprigs of parsley and lemon wedges, to garnish			
Spiced Potato Skins (see page 94) and a mixed salad, to serve			

1 Brush the steaks with oil and dust liberally with the steak seasoning.

2 Lay the prawns in a shallow dish and sprinkle with the lemon juice.

3 Mix the remaining ingredients together and chill until ready to serve.

4 Cook the steaks on the barbecue for 8–15 minutes, turning occasionally, until cooked to your liking.

5 Brush the prawns with oil and cook for 2 minutes on each side until pink and just cooked through.

6 Transfer the steaks and prawns to serving plates, garnish with sprigs of parsley and lemon wedges and serve with the caper and mustard mayonnaise, Spiced Potato Skins and a mixed salad.

Californian-style Chilli Dogs

Serves 6

	METRIC	IMPERIAL	AMERICAN
Red wine	120 ml	4 fl oz	½ cup
Sunflower oil	15 ml	1 tbsp	1 tbsp
Garlic clove, crushed	1	1	1
Juice of 1 lemon			
Made English mustard	5 ml	1 tsp	1 tsp
Tomato ketchup (catsup)	30 ml	2 tbsp	2 tbsp
Red chilli, seeded and chopped	1	1	1
Worcestershire sauce	5 ml	1 tsp	1 tsp
Clear honey	15 ml	1 tbsp	1 tbsp
Small onion, finely chopped	1	1	1
Rashers (slices) of rindless streaky bacon	6	6	6
Hot dog sausages	6	6	6
Finger rolls	6	6	6
Shredded lettuce			

1 Mix all the ingredients except the bacon, hot dogs, rolls and lettuce together in a saucepan. Bring to the boil and remove from the heat.

2 Add the hot dogs and leave to marinate for at least 1 hour, preferably longer.

3 Remove the sausages from the marinade and wrap each in a rasher of bacon. Secure with soaked wooden cocktail sticks (toothpicks).

4 Boil the remaining marinade until reduced by half.

5 Barbecue the wrapped sausages over hot coals for about 6 minutes, turning occasionally, until the bacon is golden, basting with the remaining marinade during cooking.

6 Split the rolls, not right through, and fill with shredded lettuce. Remove the cocktail sticks from the hot dogs and place the chilli dogs in the rolls. Serve straight away.

Barbecued Pork with Chilli and Cumin

Serves 4

	METRIC	IMPERIAL	AMERICAN
Cumin seeds, coarsely crushed	10 ml	2 tsp	2 tsp
Olive oil	15 ml	1 tbsp	1 tbsp
Balsamic vinegar	15 ml	1 tbsp	1 tbsp
Light soy sauce	30 ml	2 tbsp	2 tbsp
Dry white wine	90 ml	6 tbsp	6 tbsp
Small red chilli, seeded and finely chopped	1	1	1
Pork tenderloin, trimmed of any fat or sinews	450 g	1 lb	1 lb
Curly endive (frisée lettuce) and Light French Dressing (see page 126), to garnish			
Warm Potato and Lentil Salad (see page 96), to serve			

1 Whisk the cumin, oil, vinegar, soy sauce, wine and chilli together in a shallow dish. Add the pork and turn to coat completely. Cover and chill overnight, turning occasionally.

2 Cook the pork over medium coals for about 25 minutes, turning occasionally, until golden and the meat gives easily when a skewer is inserted in the thickest part. Wrap in foil and leave to rest on the side of the barbecue for 10 minutes. Cut into thick slices, lay on plates and garnish with curly endive, dressed with a little Light French Dressing and Warm Potato and Lentil Salad.

FISH

Delicious and healthy, all types of seafood make wonderful barbecue food and in California there is an abundance! All types take less time than meat to marinade and because they need no more than a quick sear over the barbecue coals they retain all their succulence and flavour.

~~~~~~~~~~~~~~~~~

Crunchy Sardines with Lemon

Serves 4–6

	METRIC	IMPERIAL	AMERICAN
Fresh sardines, cleaned and heads removed	1 kg	2¼ lb	2¼ lb
Finely grated rind and juice of 1 small lemon			
Salt and freshly ground black pepper			
Oat bran	50 g	2 oz	1 cup
Cornflakes, crushed	50 g	2 oz	1 cup
Sesame seeds	30 ml	2 tbsp	2 tbsp
Olive oil	30 ml	2 tbsp	2 tbsp
Lemon wedges and sprigs of parsley, to garnish			

1 Rinse the sardines and pat dry on kitchen paper (paper towels). Lay on a baking (cookie) sheet. Sprinkle with the lemon rind and juice and season with salt and pepper.

2 Mix the oat bran with the cornflakes and sesame seeds.

3 Brush the sardines with the oil, then coat completely in the oat bran mixture.

4 Lay the fish in an oiled, hinged wire rack (cook in two batches, if necessary).

5 Barbecue for 5–6 minutes on each side until golden and cooked through. Garnish with lemon wedges and parsley and serve.

Rustic Tuna Steaks with Garlic and Parsley

Serves 4

	METRIC	IMPERIAL	AMERICAN
Tuna steaks	4	4	4
Salt and freshly ground black pepper			
Olive oil	60 ml	4 tbsp	4 tbsp
Juice of 1 lemon			
Garlic cloves, finely chopped	2	2	2
Chopped parsley	60 ml	4 tbsp	4 tbsp
Crusty French bread and a green salad, to serve			

1 Wipe the tuna steaks and lay each on a sheet of foil, shiny side up.

2 Season lightly with salt and pepper.

3 Whisk the oil and lemon juice together and pour over. Sprinkle with the chopped garlic and parsley.

4 Wrap in the foil and seal well.

5 Barbecue over hot coals for about 12 minutes, turning once, until the tuna is cooked through.

6 Carefully transfer the steaks and their juices to warm serving plates and serve with crusty bread and a fresh green salad.

Sizzling Lobster with Citrus Fire Butter

Serves 4

	METRIC	IMPERIAL	AMERICAN
Spring (collard) greens, finely shredded	350 g	12 oz	12 oz
Oil for frying			
A little coarse sea salt			
Butter or sunflower spread	100 g	4 oz	½ cup
Finely grated rind and juice of 1 large orange			
Red chilli, seeded and finely chopped	1	1	1
Green chilli, seeded and finely chopped	1	1	1
Freshly ground black pepper			
Lobsters, about 750 g/1½ lb each	2	2	2
Sunflower oil	30 ml	2 tbsp	2 tbsp
Lemon and orange wedges, to garnish			
Jacket Potatoes (see page 93) with Soured Cream and Chive Topping (see page 128), to serve			

1   Wash and thoroughly dry the shredded greens on kitchen paper (paper towels). Deep-fry a little at a time in hot oil for 2–3 minutes until crisp (be careful because it will spit). Drain on kitchen paper. Sprinkle with sea salt and toss gently.

2   Mash the butter or spread with the orange rind and chopped chillies. Season with a little pepper.

3 Cut the lobsters into halves lengthways and remove the stomach sac from behind the head and the black vein that runs the length of the body. Brush all over with sunflower oil. Drizzle the flesh with the orange juice.

4 Place the lobsters on the barbecue, flesh-side down, and cook for 30 seconds. Turn over. Spread the butter mixture over the flesh and continue barbecuing until the butter is melted and sizzling.

5 Put the crispy greens in a layer on four serving plates. Top each with a half of lobster and garnish with orange and lemon wedges. Serve hot with Jacket Potatoes with Soured Cream and Chive Topping.

Ocean Beach Crab with Lemon Mayo

Serves 4

	METRIC	IMPERIAL	AMERICAN
Low-calorie mayonnaise	120 ml	4 fl oz	½ cup
Finely grated rind and juice of 1 large lemon			
Cans of white crabmeat, drained	2×170 g	2×6 oz	2 small
Soft fresh breadcrumbs	100 g	4 oz	2 cups
Can of pimientos, drained and chopped	200 g	7 oz	1 small
Snipped chives	30 ml	2 tbsp	2 tbsp
Chopped parsley	15 ml	1 tbsp	1 tbsp
Cayenne	1.5 ml	¼ tsp	¼ tsp
Salt and freshly ground black pepper			
A little milk			
Soured (dairy sour) cream	45 ml	3 tbsp	3 tbsp
Sunflower oil	30 ml	2 tbsp	2 tbsp
Crispy Crunch Salad (see page 113), to serve			

1 Put 90 ml/6 tbsp of the mayonnaise in a bowl with half the lemon juice. Add the crab, half the breadcrumbs, the pimientos and herbs.

2 Mix thoroughly and season to taste with the cayenne, salt and pepper. Moisten with a little milk, if necessary.

3 Shape into eight small cakes and coat in the remaining breadcrumbs. Chill until ready to cook.

4 Mix the remaining mayonnaise with the lemon rind and remaining juice, the soured cream and seasoning to taste. Chill.

5 Lay a sheet of foil on the barbecue and brush with oil. Add the crab cakes, brush with oil and turn over. Brush again. Cook for about 4 minutes on each side until browned and cooked through. Serve with the chilled lemon mayonnaise and a Crispy Crunch Salad.

Ginger-lime Salmon Fillet with Fresh Pineapple

Serves 6

	METRIC	IMPERIAL	AMERICAN
Limes	3	3	3
Sesame oil	30 ml	2 tbsp	2 tbsp
Olive oil	15 ml	1 tbsp	1 tbsp
Grated fresh root ginger	10 ml	2 tsp	2 tsp
Small garlic clove, crushed	1	1	1
Clear honey	30 ml	2 tbsp	2 tbsp
Light soy sauce	15 ml	1 tbsp	1 tbsp
Small salmon fillets, about 150 g/5 oz each, skinned	6	6	6
Small pineapple	1	1	1
Sesame seeds	30 ml	2 tbsp	2 tbsp
Snipped chives	15 ml	1 tbsp	1 tbsp
Freshly ground black pepper			
A handful of whole chives, to garnish			
Thai Fragrant Rice Moulds (see page 108), to serve			

1 Finely grate the rind from one of the limes and squeeze the juice from it and one other. Cut the remaining lime into six slices, discarding both ends.

2 Put the lime rind and juice in a large shallow container. Mix in the oils, ginger, garlic, honey and soy sauce.

3 Lay the salmon in the dish and turn to coat with the marinade. Cover and chill for 1 hour, turning once.

4 Meanwhile, cut all the skin off the pineapple and cut the flesh into six slices. Discard the tough central core.

5 Toast the sesame seeds and mix with the snipped chives.

6 Make a hole in the centre of each reserved lime slice and push a few long chives through so the lime is like a ring round the centre.

7 Lay the fish, skinned sides up, and the pineapple in a single layer on foil on the barbecue over moderate coals. Barbecue for 6 minutes until the fish is tender and the pineapple is golden, turning the pineapple once during cooking. Brush the fish with the remaining marinade during cooking.

8 Transfer the fish to serving plates. Top each with a slice of pineapple and a sprinkling of sesame seeds and snipped chives. Lay a chive and lime garnish to one side of each and serve straight away with a Thai Fragrant Rice Mould turned out on each plate.

Barbi-stewed Striped Bass with Herbs

You can use any firm-fleshed fish fillets for this recipe.

Serves 6

	METRIC	IMPERIAL	AMERICAN
Shallots, finely chopped	2	2	2
Butter or sunflower spread	15 g	½ oz	1 tbsp
Striped bass fillets, skinned and boned	1 kg	2¼ lb	2¼ lb
Dry white wine	120 ml	4 fl oz	½ cup
Chicken stock, made with ½ stock cube	150 ml	¼ pt	⅔ cup
Small lemon, cut into slices	1	1	1
Finely chopped sage	15 ml	1 tbsp	1 tbsp
Finely chopped parsley	15 ml	1 tbsp	1 tbsp
Salt and freshly ground black pepper			
Cornflour (cornstarch), blended with 30 ml/2 tbsp water	15 ml	1 tbsp	1 tbsp
Small sprigs of sage, to garnish			
Potato and Courgette Brochettes (see page 91), to serve			

1   In a flameproof shallow dish or frying pan (skillet), suitable for putting on the barbecue, fry (sauté) the shallot in butter or spread for 2 minutes, stirring, to soften. Remove from the heat.

2   Lay the fish fillets, just overlapping, on top.

3   Pour over the wine and stock. Lay the lemon slices on top and sprinkle with the herbs and a little seasoning.

4   Cover loosely with foil and cook on the barbecue for
     about 30 minutes until the fish is tender and cooked
     through. Carefully transfer to serving plates.

5   Stir the cornflour and water mixture into the juices
     and boil for 1 minute, stirring. Taste and re-season, if
     necessary. Spoon over the fish and serve garnished
     with small sprigs of sage with Potato and Courgette
     Brochettes.

Tropical-stuffed Trout

Serves 4

	METRIC	IMPERIAL	AMERICAN
Large spring (collard) greens leaves	4	4	4
Rainbow trout, cleaned	4	4	4
Juice of 1 small lime			
Light soy sauce	15 ml	1 tbsp	1 tbsp
Medium sherry	15 ml	1 tbsp	1 tbsp
Ripe avocado, peeled, stoned (pitted) and sliced	1	1	1
Slightly green banana, sliced	1	1	1
Oil for greasing			
Freshly ground black pepper			
Lime wedges, to garnish			
Wild Rice and Prawn Salad (see page 107), to serve			

1 Cut out any thick central base stalk from the leaves. Blanch the leaves in boiling water for 3 minutes. Drain, rinse with cold water and drain again.

2 Rinse the fish and pat dry with kitchen paper (paper towels). Cut off the heads, if liked. Mix the lime juice with the soy sauce and sherry and use to brush the fish inside and out.

3 Stuff the body cavities with the avocado and banana slices. Lay each leaf on a large piece of oiled foil, shiny side up. Put a fish on each leaf and drizzle with any remaining lime juice mixture. Add a good grinding of pepper. Wrap up in the leaves, then foil, to form secure parcels.

4   Barbecue over hot coals for 25 minutes, turning once after 15 minutes. Unwrap, lift the green parcels on to serving plates, garnish with lemon wedges and serve hot with a Wild Rice and Prawn Salad.

Prawn and Artichoke Kebabs

Serves 4

	METRIC	IMPERIAL	AMERICAN
Can of artichoke hearts, drained	420 g	15 oz	1 large
Raw shelled king prawns (jumbo shrimp)	16	16	16
Olive oil	30 ml	2 tbsp	2 tbsp
Lemon juice	15 ml	1 tbsp	1 tbsp
Paprika	10 ml	2 tsp	2 tsp
Freshly ground black pepper			
Lemon wedges, to garnish			
Caviar Cream (see page 135) and a mixed salad, to serve			

1   Halve the artichoke hearts and pat dry on kitchen paper (paper towels). Thread alternately with the prawns on soaked wooden skewers.

2   Whisk the oil and lemon juice together with the paprika and a little black pepper. Brush over the kebabs.

3   Barbecue for 4–6 minutes, turning occasionally and brushing with the olive oil and lemon, until golden and the prawns are cooked through. Garnish with lemon wedges and serve with Caviar Cream and a mixed salad.

Seafood Kebabs Santa Barbara

Serves 4

	METRIC	IMPERIAL	AMERICAN
Large shelled scallops	8	8	8
Thin slices of pancetta, cut in half	4	4	4
1 orange, ends removed and cut into 8 slices			
Raw shelled king prawns (jumbo shrimp)	8	8	8
1 lemon, ends removed and cut into 8 slices			
Monkfish, cut into 8 cubes	175 g	6 oz	6 oz
Olive oil	15 ml	1 tbsp	1 tbsp
Balsamic vinegar	15 ml	1 tbsp	1 tbsp
Finely chopped black olives	15 ml	1 tbsp	1 tbsp
Small onion, finely chopped	1	1	1
Chopped parsley	15 ml	1 tbsp	1 tbsp
Garlic and Herb Baguette (see page 122) and Melon, Cucumber and Tomato Salad (see page 112), to serve			

1 Roll each scallop in half a slice of pancetta. Thread one on each of four soaked wooden skewers. Then add a slice of orange to each. Slide on a prawn, then a slice of lemon, then a cube of monkfish.

2 Repeat the threading, to complete the four kebabs.

3 Mix the oil and balsamic vinegar together and brush over the kebabs. Barbecue over moderate coals for 4–6 minutes until cooked through and lightly golden, brushing with more oil and vinegar during cooking.

4 Mix together the olives, onion and parsley. Transfer the kebabs to serving plates and sprinkle with the olive mixture before serving with a Garlic and Herb Baguette and Melon, Cucumber and Tomato Salad.

Summer Waters Swordfish Steaks

Serves 4

	METRIC	IMPERIAL	AMERICAN
Swordfish steaks	4	4	4
Chinese five spice powder	15 ml	1 tbsp	1 tbsp
Sesame oil	60 ml	4 tbsp	4 tbsp
Lemon juice	30 ml	2 tbsp	2 tbsp
Beansprouts	100 g	4 oz	2 cups
Red (bell) pepper, finely shredded	1	1	1
Spring onions (scallions), finely sliced	2	2	2
Light soy sauce			
Jacket Potatoes (see page 93) with Prawn Topping (see page 129), to serve			

1   Wipe the fish with kitchen paper (paper towels) and remove the skin.

2   Mix the five spice powder with half the oil and half the lemon juice. Brush all over the fish and leave to marinate for 2 hours.

3   Mix the beansprouts with the pepper and spring onion. Whisk together the soy sauce with the remaining oil and lemon juice.

4   Barbecue the fish over hot coals for 3–4 minutes on each side, turning once and brushing with any remaining marinade, until cooked through.

5 Add the soy dressing to the beansprout mixture. Toss gently. Spoon on to serving plates.

6 Transfer the swordfish to the plates and serve with Jacket Potatoes with Prawn Topping.

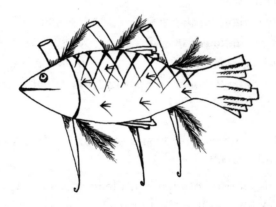

Mackerel with Horseradish

Serves 4

	METRIC	IMPERIAL	AMERICAN
Mackerel, cleaned	4	4	4
Sprigs of thyme	4	4	4
Sunflower oil	30 ml	2 tbsp	2 tbsp
Horseradish sauce	30 ml	2 tbsp	2 tbsp
Lemon juice	5 ml	1 tsp	1 tsp
A pinch of salt			
Freshly ground black pepper			
Butter or sunflower spread	50 g	2 oz	¼ cup
Chopped parsley	30 ml	2 tbsp	2 tbsp
Smokey Baby Potatoes (see page 92) and French Bean Salad (see page 104), to serve			

1 Wash the fish inside and out and pat dry with kitchen paper (paper towels).

2 Push a sprig of thyme inside the body cavity of each. Lay the fish in a shallow dish.

3 Mix the oil with half the horseradish, the lemon juice, salt and lots of pepper.

4 Pour over the fish, turn to coat completely and leave to marinate in a cool place for at least 2 hours.

5 Remove from the marinade and lay in a hinged wire rack.

6 Barbecue for 10–15 minutes, turning once and brushing with any remaining marinade, until cooked through.

7 Meanwhile, put the butter or spread in a small saucepan with the remaining horseradish, parsley and a good grinding of pepper. Heat on the side of the barbecue until melted, stirring to blend.

8 Transfer the cooked fish to serving plates and spoon the horseradish sauce over. Serve with Smokey Baby Potatoes and French Bean Salad.

Salmon Santa Rosa

Serves 6

	METRIC	IMPERIAL	AMERICAN
Butter, softened, or sunflower spread	50 g	2 oz	¼ cup
Salmon fillets, about 175 g/6 oz each, skinned	6	6	6
Finely grated rind and juice of 1 small lemon			
A pinch of salt			
Freshly ground black pepper			
Button mushrooms, sliced	175 g	6 oz	6 oz
Bunch of spring onions (scallions), chopped	1	1	1
Capers	30 ml	2 tbsp	2 tbsp
Chopped parsley	30 ml	2 tbsp	2 tbsp
Dried marjoram	5 ml	1 tsp	1 tsp
Soured (dairy sour) cream	150 ml	¼ pt	⅔ cup
Jar of red lumpfish roe	50 g	2 oz	1 small

1 Smear six sheets of foil with some of the butter or sunflower spread. Lay a salmon fillet on each.

2 Sprinkle with the lemon rind and juice, seasoning, the mushrooms, onions, capers, parsley and marjoram.

3 Dot with the remaining butter or spread, fold the foil over the ingredients and tightly roll the edges together.

4 Cook over hot coals for 12–15 minutes, turning once.

5 Open the foil on serving plates and top with a spoonful each of soured cream and lumpfish roe.

VEGETARIAN DISHES

With so many wonderful influences from all over the world, Californians are well-placed to create sensational barbecues without any meat or fish. A huge variety of fabulous fresh fruit and vegetables is readily available and with the addition of some stunning cheeses and a few hearty pulses, it's easy to enjoy a meat-free barbecue, Californian-style.

Marinated Mushroom and Chestnut Kebabs

Serves 4

	METRIC	IMPERIAL	AMERICAN
Button mushrooms, stalks trimmed	225 g	8 oz	8 oz
Can of whole water chestnuts, drained	230 g	8 oz	1 small
Bunch of fat-bulbed spring onions (scallions)	1	1	1
Red (bell) pepper, cut into chunks	1	1	1
Green pepper, cut into chunks	1	1	1
Light soy sauce	60 ml	4 tbsp	4 tbsp
Medium sherry	75 ml	5 tbsp	5 tbsp
Garlic clove, crushed	1	1	1
Clear honey	5 ml	1 tsp	1 tsp
Grated fresh root ginger	2.5 ml	½ tsp	½ tsp
Oriental Soya Bean Salad (see page 106), to serve			

1 Put the mushrooms and drained water chestnuts in a large shallow dish.

2 Trim the roots and tops from the spring onions, leaving most of the green intact. Add to the dish with the peppers.

3 Whisk the soy sauce with the sherry, garlic, honey and ginger. Pour into the dish and toss the ingredients together to coat completely. Cover and leave to marinate overnight, turning occasionally.

4 Thread the mushrooms, water chestnuts, red and green peppers alternately on soaked wooden cocktail sticks (toothpicks). Lay with the spring onions on a sheet of foil. Barbecue for about 6 minutes, turning occasionally and brushing with any remaining marinade during cooking, until the mushrooms and peppers are tender and the onions are turning golden.

5 Serve the kebabs and the onions with an Oriental Soya Bean Salad.

Monterey Jack Green Broil

Serves 4–6

	METRIC	IMPERIAL	AMERICAN
Wild rice mix	175 g	6 oz	¾ cup
Onion, finely chopped	1	1	1
Butter or sunflower spread, plus a little for greasing	25 g	1 oz	2 tbsp
Frozen chopped spinach, thawed	450 g	1 lb	1 lb
Monterey Jack cheese, grated	225 g	8 oz	2 cups
Dijon mustard	5 ml	1 tsp	1 tsp
Chopped hazelnuts (filberts)	50 g	2 oz	½ cup
Egg, beaten	1	1	1
Salt and freshly ground black pepper			
Barbecue Sauce (see page 132) and Crispy Crunch Salad (see page 113), to serve			

1 Cook the wild rice mix according to the packet directions. Drain, rinse with cold water and drain again.

2 Fry (sauté) the onion in the butter or spread for 2 minutes, stirring. Tip into the rice.

3 Squeeze the spinach thoroughly to remove all excess moisture. Add to the rice with all the remaining ingredients, seasoning to taste with salt and pepper.

4 Shape into a roll on a large piece of well-greased foil, shiny side up. Roll up and twist the ends securely. Chill until ready to cook.

5 Barbecue over moderate coals for about 40 minutes, turning occasionally, until set and cooked through. Serve sliced with a helping of Barbecue Sauce and a Crispy Crunch Salad.

Three Cheese Raclette

This is a guest participation dish! Everyone needs to come up to the barbecue, to take a little of the cheeses as they melt.

Serves 6

	METRIC	IMPERIAL	AMERICAN
Piece of Monterey Jack cheese	*225 g*	*8 oz*	*8 oz*
Piece of Emmental (Swiss) cheese	*225 g*	*8 oz*	*8 oz*
Piece of Muenster or Cheddar cheese	*225 g*	*8 oz*	*8 oz*
A selection of crackers, small squares of rye bread and French toast			
Cooked baby new potatoes and Californian Pickled Vegetables (see page 110), to serve			

1 Trim the cheeses of any rind and put them in three separate shallow roasting tins (pans) or metal dishes.

2 Place the containers on the side of the barbecue, with the thickest end of the cheeses nearest the coals. As the cheese melts, guests scrape off the melted part on to crackers, rye bread and French toast. Serve with a bowl of cooked baby new potatoes and Californian Pickled Vegetables.

Huevos Rancheros

Serves 4

	METRIC	IMPERIAL	AMERICAN
Fairly fat aubergines (eggplants)	2	2	2
Salt			
Olive oil			
Tomatoes, skinned and chopped	2	2	2
Shallot, finely chopped	1	1	1
Garlic clove, crushed	1	1	1
Lemon juice, to taste			
Freshly ground black pepper			
Passata (sieved tomatoes)	60 ml	4 tbsp	4 tbsp
Mozzarella cheese, grated	50 g	2 oz	½ cup
Small eggs	4	4	4
Chopped basil	30 ml	2 tbsp	2 tbsp

1 Trim the stalk ends off the aubergines and discard. Boil in lightly salted water for about 15 minutes until tender. Drain, rinse with cold water and drain again.

2 Cut into halves lengthways and scoop out most of the flesh, leaving a fairly thick border all round.

3 Brush all over with olive oil and place on a baking (cookie) sheet. Alternatively, lay each aubergine shell on a double thickness of foil and mould around the shell to form a container.

4 Chop the scooped-out flesh finely and place in a bowl.

5 Add the tomatoes, shallot and garlic. Gradually whisk in 60 ml/4 tbsp olive oil, a little at a time, until a thick, rough paste is formed. Spike with lemon juice and season with pepper. Cover and chill.

6 Divide the passata among the aubergine shells. Top with the cheese. Press down gently in the centre of the cheese to form a small well.

7 Break an egg into each and season with pepper.

8 Cook on the barbecue for about 20 minutes or until the eggs are set to your liking.

9 Transfer to serving plates, sprinkle with the basil and serve with the aubergine salsa.

Cracked Wheat Patty and Aubergine Sandwiches

Serves 4

	METRIC	IMPERIAL	AMERICAN
Small aubergines (eggplants)	2	2	2
Salt			
Water	1 litre	1¾ pts	4¼ cups
Cornmeal	100 g	4 oz	1 cup
Peanut butter	15 ml	1 tbsp	1 tbsp
Freshly ground black pepper			
Salted peanuts, finely chopped	75 g	3 oz	¾ cup
Bulgar (cracked wheat)	175 g	6 oz	1 cup
Garlic clove, crushed	1	1	1
Chopped parsley	30 ml	2 tbsp	2 tbsp
A good pinch of cayenne			
Olive oil for brushing			
Passata (sieved tomatoes)	200 ml	7 fl oz	scant 1 cup
Dried oregano	2.5 ml	½ tsp	½ tsp
Clear honey	10 ml	2 tsp	2 tsp
Spinach, Cucumber and Kiwi Salad (see page 114), to serve			

1 Cut the stalks off the aubergines and discard. Then cut the aubergines, lengthways, into four thick slices.

2 Sprinkle with salt, place in a colander and leave to stand while preparing the patties.

3 Bring 500 ml/17 fl oz/2¼ cups of the water to the boil in a large pan. Add the cornmeal, peanut butter and a little seasoning. Cook, stirring frequently, over a very gentle heat for about 3 minutes until the mixture is very thick and leaves the sides of the pan clean. Stir in the peanuts and leave to cool.

4 Put the bulgar in a separate heavy pan and cook gently, stirring as it heats, for about 4 minutes until lightly toasted. Add the remaining water, bring to the boil, cover the pan, reduce the heat and simmer for about 20 minutes, stirring occasionally to prevent sticking. Season with salt and pepper.

5 Using your hands, work the two mixtures together with the garlic, parsley and cayenne. Shape into four flat, oval patties, just smaller than the aubergine slices. Chill well.

6 Rinse the aubergine slices and pat dry with kitchen paper (paper towels). Brush all over with oil. Brush the patties with oil and place in a hinged wire rack.

7 Mix the passata with the oregano and honey in a small saucepan and season lightly. Heat at the side of the barbecue.

8 Barbecue the patties and aubergine slices for about 10 minutes, turning occasionally, until golden. Transfer four of the aubergine slices to four serving plates. Top each with a patty, then another aubergine slice. Spoon a little of the warm passata sauce over and serve with a Spinach, Cucumber and Kiwi Salad.

Grilled Polenta with Cheese and Italian Tomatoes

You can buy instant polenta. It doesn't have such a good flavour but it is quicker – it will take only 1 minute to cook.

Serves 4

	METRIC	IMPERIAL	AMERICAN
Water	900 ml	1½ pts	3¾ cups
A good pinch of salt			
Polenta	225 g	8 oz	2 cups
Butter or sunflower spread	75 g	3 oz	⅓ cup
Parmesan cheese, grated	50 g	2 oz	½ cup
Beefsteak tomatoes	4	4	4
Freshly ground black pepper			
Mozzarella cheese, grated	100 g	4 oz	1 cup
Pesto from a jar	60 ml	4 tbsp	4 tbsp
Olive oil for brushing			
Sprigs of basil, to garnish			
Ciabatta bread and a mixed green salad, to serve			

1 Bring the water and salt to the boil. Gradually add the polenta in a thin stream and stir until the mixture begins to thicken.

2 Reduce the heat and cook gently, stirring occasionally, for about 20 minutes until really thick.

3 Stir in the butter or spread and cheese and turn into an oiled Swiss roll tin (jelly roll pan), spreading out so that the mixture is about 2.5 cm/1 in thick. Leave to cool, then chill.

4 Cut a slice off the rounded end of each tomato (they will stand up on the stalk ends). Scoop out the seeds and discard. Season the insides with pepper.

5 Divide the cheese among the tomatoes, then top each with a spoonful of pesto. Replace the 'lids' and wrap each tomato in oiled foil.

6 Cut the polenta into squares and brush these with oil.

7 Stand the tomatoes on the barbecue rack and add the polenta squares. Cook for 10 minutes, turning the squares once, until they are golden brown and the tomatoes are hot through but not completely soft.

8 Carefully unwrap the tomatoes and transfer to warmed serving plates with the polenta. Garnish with sprigs of basil and serve with ciabatta bread and a mixed green salad.

Pizza on the Coals

Serves 4

	METRIC	IMPERIAL	AMERICAN
Self-raising (self-rising) flour	225 g	8 oz	2 cups
A pinch of salt			
Margarine	50 g	2 oz	¼ cup
Cold water, to mix			
Sunflower or olive oil for brushing			
Tomato purée (paste)	100 g	4 oz	4 oz
Tomatoes, thinly sliced	3	3	3
Mozzarella cheese, grated	225 g	8 oz	2 cups
Dried oregano	5 ml	1 tsp	1 tsp
A few black olives, stoned (pitted)			

1 Put the flour and salt in a bowl and rub in the margarine. Mix with enough water to form a soft but not sticky dough.

2 Divide into four equal portions and flatten out to 15 cm/6 in rounds.

3 Lay a sheet of foil on the barbecue rack and brush with oil. Add the dough rounds and barbecue for about 3 minutes, until browning underneath. Brush the surface with oil and turn over.

4 Spread with the tomato purée, top with the tomato slices, then the cheese. Sprinkle with oregano and dot with a few olives. Cover loosely with another piece of foil and cook for 10 minutes until the cheese has melted. Serve straight away.

Hot 'n' Tasty Quorn Steaks

Serves 4

	METRIC	IMPERIAL	AMERICAN
Quorn steaks	4	4	4
Golden (light corn) syrup	15 ml	1 tbsp	1 tbsp
Tomato purée (paste)	30 ml	2 tbsp	2 tbsp
A pinch of Chinese five spice powder			
Red wine vinegar	15 ml	1 tbsp	1 tbsp
Freshly ground black pepper			
Tabasco sauce, to taste			
Beansprouts	100 g	4 oz	2 cups
Small green (bell) pepper, very thinly sliced	1	1	1
Hot Barbecued Noodles (see page 97), to serve			

1 Lay the quorn steaks in a shallow dish in a single layer.

2 Mix together all the remaining ingredients except the beansprouts and pepper.

3 Spoon over the steaks and leave to marinate for at least 2 hours, turning once or twice.

4 Remove from the marinade and barbecue for 8–10 minutes, turning once or twice and brushing with any remaining marinade, until cooked and richly coated in the marinade.

5 Mix the beansprouts and pepper together. Transfer the steaks to serving plates, garnish with the beansprout mixture and serve with Hot Barbecued Noodles.

Smoked Tofu and Asparagus Kebabs with Poached Walnuts

For a change, use plain tofu and brush with bottled barbecue sauce before cooking.

Serves 4

	METRIC	IMPERIAL	AMERICAN
Walnut halves	100 g	4 oz	1 cup
Vegetable stock, made with ½ stock cube	150 ml	¼ pt	⅔ cup
Walnut oil	30 ml	2 tbsp	2 tbsp
A squeeze of lemon juice			
A pinch of chilli powder			
A pinch of caster (superfine) sugar			
Thick asparagus spears	225 g	8 oz	8 oz
Smoked tofu cubes	450 g	1 lb	1 lb
Lemon, cut into thick slices	1	1	1
Butter or sunflower spread, melted	50 g	2 oz	¼ cup
Freshly ground black pepper			
Curly endive (frisée lettuce), to garnish			
Smokey Baby Potatoes (see page 92), to serve			

1 Put the walnut halves in a saucepan suitable for putting on the barbecue later. Add the stock, walnut oil, lemon juice, chilli powder and sugar. Bring to the boil, reduce the heat and simmer, stirring occasionally, until the liquid has almost evaporated and the walnuts are just coated in sauce.

2 Cut the asparagus into thick chunks. Blanch in boiling water for 2 minutes. Drain. Thread on soaked wooden skewers with the tofu and lemon slices. Brush with melted butter or sunflower spread and season with pepper.

3 Barbecue for about 10 minutes, turning occasionally until golden brown, brushing with more melted butter or spread during cooking.

4 Heat the walnut halves at the side of the barbecue.

5 Transfer the kebabs to serving plates. Spoon the walnut halves to one side. Garnish with curly endive and serve with Smokey Baby Potatoes.

Camembert Crunch with Cranberry Beans

Use Brie instead of Camembert, if you prefer.

Serves 4

	METRIC	IMPERIAL	AMERICAN
Individual wedges of Camembert, well chilled	8	8	8
Egg, beaten	1	1	1
Packet of Country Herb stuffing mix	85 g	3½ oz	1 small
Fresh cranberries	100 g	4 oz	4 oz
Water	45 ml	3 tbsp	3 tbsp
Light brown sugar	30 ml	2 tbsp	2 tbsp
Can of red kidney beans	425 g	15 oz	1 large
Snipped chives	30 ml	2 tbsp	2 tbsp
Freshly ground black pepper			
Sunflower oil for brushing			
Sprigs of parsley, to garnish			
Crusty bread and a mixed salad, to serve			

1   Dip the Camembert wedges in beaten egg, then in the stuffing mix. Repeat until the cheeses are thoroughly covered. Chill until ready to cook.

2   Put the cranberries in a saucepan suitable for transferring to the barbecue. Add the water. Cook until the fruit starts to pop. Add the sugar and simmer for 5 minutes, stirring occasionally.

3   Drain the beans, rinse with cold water and drain again. Add to the cranberries and mix gently but thoroughly. Stir in the chives and season with pepper.

4 Brush a double thickness of foil liberally with oil. Place on the barbecue rack. Put the pan of cranberries and beans on the barbecue to heat through. Cook the cheeses for about 4 minutes, turning occasionally, until crisp and golden.

5 Transfer the cheeses to warm serving plates. Spoon the bean mixture to one side. Garnish with parsley and serve with crusty bread and a mixed salad.

Acorn Squash with Green Garlic and Herb Custard

Serves 4

	METRIC	IMPERIAL	AMERICAN
Acorn squash	2	2	2
Butter or sunflower spread, melted	50 g	2 oz	¼ cup
Garlic and herb soft cheese	100 g	4 oz	½ cup
Finely chopped parsley	15 ml	1 tbsp	1 tbsp
Finely chopped watercress	15 ml	1 tbsp	1 tbsp
Small eggs	2	2	2
Small sprigs of watercress, to garnish			
Sweet Potato Butterhorns (see page 118) or crusty bread and French Bean Salad (see page 104), to serve			

1   Cut the squashes into halves and scoop out the seeds. Cook in boiling, lightly salted water or steam for about 15 minutes until the flesh feels just tender. Drain and dry on kitchen paper (paper towels). Brush with a little of the melted butter or spread.

2   Whisk the cheese, parsley, watercress and eggs together until well blended.

3   When ready to cook, put the squash halves on the barbecue, cut sides down, and cook for about 5 minutes until turning golden. Turn over.

4   Spoon the cheese mixture into the cavities and drizzle with the remaining butter or spread. Cook for about 15 minutes or until the custard is set.

5   Garnish each with watercress and serve with Sweet Potato Butterhorns and a French Bean Salad.

SALADS AND SIDE DISHES

It's the little extras that turn a good barbecue into a great one. Many of these hot side dishes can be started in the kitchen and then finished off over the coals. The salads, of course, can be made in advance, then kept cool until ready to serve. These recipes are specifically designed to complement the main courses in the book but are also the ideal accompaniments to any plain barbecued fish, meat or poultry.

Lemon Glazed Potatoes

Serves 4–6

	METRIC	IMPERIAL	AMERICAN
Potatoes, thickly sliced	1 kg	2¼ lb	2¼ lb
Salt			
Butter or sunflower spread	50 g	2 oz	¼ cup
Olive oil	45 ml	3 tbsp	3 tbsp
Clear honey	60 ml	4 tbsp	4 tbsp
Finely grated rind and juice of ½ lemon			
Dried basil	5 ml	1 tsp	1 tsp
Freshly ground black pepper			

1 Cook the potatoes in boiling, lightly salted water for 5 minutes. Drain.

2 Heat the remaining ingredients in a roasting tin (pan) on the barbecue. Add the potato slices, turn to coat in the mixture. Cook on the barbecue for about 10 minutes, turning occasionally, until cooked through, browned and stickily glazed.

Potato and Courgette Brochettes

Serves 4

	METRIC	IMPERIAL	AMERICAN
Bay leaves	8	8	8
Baby potatoes, scrubbed	16	16	16
Button (pearl) onions, peeled but left whole	16	16	16
Salt			
Large courgettes (zucchini), each cut into 8 chunks	2	2	2
Olive oil	15 ml	1 tbsp	1 tbsp
Garlic clove, crushed	1	1	1

1 Soak the bay leaves in cold water while preparing the vegetables (it helps prevent them from burning during cooking).

2 Cook the potatoes and onions in boiling, lightly salted water for 6 minutes until partially softened. Add the courgettes halfway through cooking. Drain, rinse with cold water and drain again.

3 Thread the vegetables alternately on eight soaked wooden skewers, adding a bay leaf halfway through the threading.

4 Whisk the oil and garlic together and brush over the vegetables. Barbecue for 10–15 minutes, turning occasionally and brushing with the oil, until golden and cooked through.

Smokey Baby Potatoes

Serves 4

	METRIC	IMPERIAL	AMERICAN
Baby potatoes, scrubbed	450 g	1 lb	1 lb
Salt and freshly ground black pepper			
Butter or sunflower spread	25 g	1 oz	2 tbsp
Smokey-flavoured barbecue sauce	30 ml	2 tbsp	2 tbsp

1 Boil the potatoes in lightly salted water for 6 minutes until almost tender. Drain.

2 Place on a large sheet of foil, shiny side up. Sprinkle with pepper, dot with the butter or spread and drizzle with the sauce.

3 Wrap the potatoes tightly in the foil to make a large parcel, taking care to seal the edges well.

4 Barbecue over hot coals for about 20 minutes, turning the parcel once, until cooked through. Serve hot.

Jacket Potatoes

Serves 4

	METRIC	IMPERIAL	AMERICAN
Large potatoes, scrubbed	4	4	4
Sunflower oil			
Salt			
Butter, sunflower spread or potato toppings (see pages 128–31), to serve			

1 Score the potatoes round the middle with a sharp knife, then prick with a fork to prevent splitting.

2 Cook the potatoes in boiling water for 15 minutes until almost tender. Drain.

3 Brush with oil and rub with salt. Wrap in foil, shiny side in.

4 Cook on the barbecue for about 30 minutes, turning occasionally, until they feel soft when squeezed with an oven-gloved hand.

5 Unwrap the foil slightly and make a cross-cut in each potato. Gently squeeze to open slightly and add a knob of butter or sunflower spread or a dollop of potato topping.

Spiced Potato Skins

Serves 6

	METRIC	IMPERIAL	AMERICAN
Large potatoes, scrubbed	6	6	6
Sunflower oil	45 ml	3 tbsp	3 tbsp
Garlic salt	5 ml	1 tsp	1 tsp
Chilli powder	5 ml	1 tsp	1 tsp
Mixed (apple-pie) spice	5 ml	1 tsp	1 tsp
Freshly ground black pepper			

1   Prick the potatoes all over with a fork. Bake in the oven at 180°C/350°F/gas mark 4 for about 1 hour or until soft. Alternatively, bake in the microwave for about 4 minutes per potato (or according to the manufacturer's directions).

2   Cut the potatoes into halves and scoop out most of the potato (reserve for a recipe needing mashed potato, if liked), leaving a wall about 5 mm/¼ in thick. Cut each half into three wedges.

3   Brush all over with oil. Mix the remaining ingredients together, then sprinkle evenly over the potato skins.

4   Barbecue for 3–4 minutes on each side until crisp and golden. Serve hot.

Barbecue Pilaf

Serves 6

	METRIC	IMPERIAL	AMERICAN
Packet of mushroom or vegetable savoury rice	120 g	4½ oz	1 small
Button mushrooms, sliced	50 g	2 oz	2 oz
Paprika	5 ml	1 tsp	1 tsp
Water			

1 Empty the rice into the centre of a 45 cm/18 in square of double-thickness foil. Draw up the sides to form a container.

2 Add the mushrooms and paprika, then carefully add the amount of water stated on the rice packet. Draw the edges of the foil together and twist to seal completely.

3 Cook over hot coals for 25 minutes. Open the parcel, fluff up with a fork and serve.

Warm Potato and Lentil Salad

Serves 4

	METRIC	IMPERIAL	AMERICAN
Brown lentils, soaked in water for 2 hours and drained	100 g	4 oz	⅔ cup
Vegetable stock, made with 1 stock cube	600 ml	1 pt	2½ cups
Small bay leaf	1	1	1
Small new potatoes, scrubbed and halved	350 g	12 oz	12 oz
Celery sticks, finely chopped	2	2	2
Spring onions (scallions), chopped	2	2	2
Light soy sauce	45 ml	3 tbsp	3 tbsp
White wine vinegar	45 ml	3 tbsp	3 tbsp
Sunflower oil	45 ml	3 tbsp	3 tbsp
Chopped parsley, to garnish			

1   Put the drained lentils in a saucepan with the stock and bay leaf. Bring to the boil, reduce the heat, cover and cook gently for 30 minutes or until tender and most of the liquid has been absorbed.

2   Cook the potatoes in boiling water in a separate pan for about 15 minutes or until just tender. Drain.

3   Add the potatoes to the lentils with the remaining ingredients and toss well. Cover the pan with foil, then a lid, and leave to one side of the barbecue (not directly over the coals) while cooking the main course. Serve warm, sprinkled with chopped parsley.

Hot Barbecued Noodles

Serves 4

	METRIC	IMPERIAL	AMERICAN
Chinese egg noodles	200 g	7 oz	2 slabs
Sunflower oil	60 ml	4 tbsp	4 tbsp
Garlic clove, peeled but left whole	1	1	1
Slice of bread, cut into very small dice	1	1	1
Poppy seeds	15 ml	1 tbsp	1 tbsp

1 Cook the noodles according to the packet directions.
Drain and reserve.

2 Heat the oil in a saucepan suitable for putting on the
barbecue. Add the garlic and bread cubes and cook,
stirring, until the bread is crisp and golden. Remove
from the heat. Take out the garlic and discard. Add
the poppy seeds.

3 When ready to serve, put the pan on the barbecue
until sizzling. Add the cooked noodles and toss
quickly for about 2–3 minutes until hot. Serve.

Sweet Parmesan Onions

Serves 6

	METRIC	IMPERIAL	AMERICAN
Spanish onions, peeled and halved	3	3	3
Butter or sunflower spread	40 g	1½ oz	3 tbsp
Caster (superfine) sugar	15 ml	1 tbsp	1 tbsp
Parmesan cheese, freshly grated	50 g	2 oz	½ cup
Celery salt	5 ml	1 tsp	1 tsp
Freshly ground black pepper			
Round lettuce leaves, to garnish	6	6	6

1 Cook the onions in boiling water for 5 minutes. Drain.

2 Smear a little butter or spread on six squares of foil, shiny sides up.

3 Put an onion half in the centre of each. Sprinkle with the sugar, cheese and celery salt. Add a good grinding of pepper to each. Turn over a couple of times to coat fairly evenly with the mixture. Dot with the remaining butter or spread.

4 Wrap securely. Barbecue for about 30 minutes until the onions are completely soft.

5 Open the parcels and carefully transfer the onions to lettuce leaves. Serve straight away.

Char-grilled Corn Cobs with Orange Butter

Serves 4

	METRIC	IMPERIAL	AMERICAN
Sweetcorn (corn) cobs in their husks	4	4	4
Finely grated rind and juice of 1 orange			
Butter or sunflower spread	50 g	2 oz	¼ cup
Freshly ground black pepper			
Chopped parsley	30 ml	2 tbsp	2 tbsp

1 Carefully pull back the husks without breaking them off and pull off the silks.

2 Brush the sweetcorn with the orange juice, then replace the husks in their original positions.

3 Put the orange rind, the butter or spread, lots of pepper and the parsley in a small saucepan. Heat at the side of the barbecue.

4 Barbecue the corn over hot coals for about 20 minutes, turning occasionally.

5 Peel off the husks and serve with the orange butter drizzled over.

99

Courgette and Mozzarella Ribbon Salad

Serves 4

	METRIC	IMPERIAL	AMERICAN
Good-sized courgettes (zucchini)	4	4	4
Mozzarella cheese	50 g	2 oz	2 oz
Olive oil	45 ml	3 tbsp	3 tbsp
White onion, thinly sliced	1	1	1
Garlic clove, crushed	1	1	1
White wine vinegar	15 ml	1 tbsp	1 tbsp
A pinch of salt			
Freshly ground black pepper			
Cherry tomatoes, halved	8	8	8
Black olives, stoned (pitted)	12	12	12
Chopped basil	15 ml	1 tbsp	1 tbsp

1 Cut off the tops and bases of the courgettes. Place the vegetables in a bowl. Cover with boiling water and leave to stand for 5 minutes. Drain and dry on kitchen paper (paper towels).

2 Using a potato peeler, pare the courgettes into thin ribbons. Place in a salad bowl.

3 Cut the Mozzarella into thin strips and add to the bowl.

4 Heat the oil in a frying pan (skillet) and cook the onion and garlic gently for 1 minute only. Remove from the heat and stir in the vinegar, salt and pepper.

5   Add the tomatoes and olives to the bowl. Spoon the
    onion mixture over and toss gently.

6   Sprinkle with the basil, toss again and serve.

Rocket, Grapefruit and Walnut Salad

Serves 4

	METRIC	IMPERIAL	AMERICAN
Pink grapefruit	2	2	2
Walnut halves	50 g	2 oz	½ cup
Rocket leaves	100 g	4 oz	4 oz
Olive oil	30 ml	2 tbsp	2 tbsp
Walnut oil	15 ml	1 tbsp	1 tbsp
White wine vinegar	15 ml	1 tbsp	1 tbsp
Clear honey	5 ml	1 tsp	1 tsp
Salt and freshly ground black pepper			

1   Hold the grapefruit over a bowl to catch the juice and
    cut off all the skin and pith with a serrated-edged
    knife. Cut both sides of each membrane and remove
    the segments. Put the segments to one side. Squeeze
    the membranes over the bowl to extract any
    remaining juice, then discard.

2   Mix the walnut halves and rocket leaves in a salad
    bowl. Arrange the grapefruit segments on top.

3   Add the remaining ingredients to the grapefruit juice
    and whisk well. Drizzle over the salad and serve.

Japanese Salad

Serves 4

	METRIC	IMPERIAL	AMERICAN
Long-grain rice	175 g	6 oz	¾ cup
Salt			
Can of anchovy fillets, drained	50 g	2 oz	1 small
Milk	30 ml	2 tbsp	2 tbsp
Small button mushrooms, thinly sliced	75 g	3 oz	3 oz
Carrot, cut into short, very fine matchsticks	1	1	1
Celery stick, cut into short, very fine matchsticks	1	1	1
Piece of cucumber, cut into short, very fine matchsticks	5 cm	2 in	2 in
Light soy sauce	30 ml	2 tbsp	2 tbsp
White wine vinegar	30 ml	2 tbsp	2 tbsp
Sesame oil	30 ml	2 tbsp	2 tbsp
Toasted sesame seeds	15 ml	1 tbsp	1 tbsp
Chopped coriander (cilantro)	15 ml	1 tbsp	1 tbsp

1 Rinse the rice, drain, then cook in boiling, lightly salted water according to the packet directions until just tender. Drain, rinse with cold water and drain again.

2 Meanwhile, soak the anchovies in the milk.

3 Put the rice in a salad bowl. Add the mushrooms, carrot, celery and cucumber and toss gently.

4   Whisk the soy sauce, vinegar and oil together and pour over the salad. Toss.

5   Sprinkle with the sesame seeds and coriander.

6   Pat the anchovies dry on kitchen paper (paper towels). Roll each one up and arrange attractively over the surface of the salad.

Tomato and Onion Salad

Serves 4

	METRIC	IMPERIAL	AMERICAN
Plum or other sweet ripe tomatoes, thinly sliced	6	6	6
Red onion, thinly sliced and separated into rings	1	1	1
Chopped parsley	30 ml	2 tbsp	2 tbsp
Chopped sage	5 ml	1 tsp	1 tsp
Olive oil	30 ml	2 tbsp	2 tbsp
Red wine vinegar	15 ml	1 tbsp	1 tbsp
A pinch of caster sugar			
Salt and freshly ground black pepper			

1   Arrange the tomatoes attractively in a shallow serving dish. Scatter the onion rings over.

2   Whisk the remaining ingredients together and drizzle over. Chill for at least 30 minutes to allow the flavours to develop.

French Bean Salad

Serves 4

	METRIC	IMPERIAL	AMERICAN
French (green) beans	225 g	8 oz	8 oz
Spring onion (scallion), finely chopped	1	1	1
Can of flageolet beans, rinsed, and drained	425 g	15 oz	1 large
Chopped parsley	15 ml	1 tbsp	1 tbsp
Chopped thyme	15 ml	1 tbsp	1 tbsp
Small garlic clove, crushed	1	1	1
Olive oil	45 ml	3 tbsp	3 tbsp
White wine vinegar	15 ml	1 tbsp	1 tbsp
Salt and freshly ground black pepper			

1 Top and tail the French beans and cut into short lengths. Cook in boiling water for 4 minutes until just tender but still with some bite. Drain, rinse with cold water and drain again.

2 Mix with the spring onion, flageolet beans and herbs.

3 Whisk the garlic with the oil, vinegar and some salt and pepper. Drizzle over the salad, toss and chill for at least 30 minutes to allow the flavours to develop.

Conchiglie Mexicano

Serves 4

	METRIC	IMPERIAL	AMERICAN
Multi-coloured conchiglie pasta	100 g	4 oz	4 oz
Can of sweetcorn (corn), drained	200 g	7 oz	1 small
Small green (bell) pepper, finely chopped	1	1	1
Stuffed olives, sliced	8	8	8
Chilli oil	15 ml	1 tbsp	1 tbsp
Sunflower oil	15 ml	1 tbsp	1 tbsp
Red wine vinegar	15 ml	1 tbsp	1 tbsp
Salt and freshly ground black pepper			
Cherry tomatoes	8	8	8
Small sprigs of coriander (cilantro)			

1   Cook the pasta according to the packet directions. Drain, rinse with cold water and drain again. Turn into a salad bowl.

2   Add the corn, pepper and olives.

3   Whisk the chilli oil and sunflower oil together with the wine vinegar and a little salt and pepper. Pour over the salad and toss gently.

4   Make three cross-cuts in the tomatoes from the rounded ends, not quite through the stalk end. Gently ease back the flesh around the seeds to resemble flower heads.

5   Arrange around the top of the salad and garnish with small sprigs of coriander.

Oriental Soya Bean Salad

Serves 4

	METRIC	IMPERIAL	AMERICAN
Can of soya beans, rinsed and drained	425g	15 oz	1 large
Beansprouts	100 g	4 oz	2 cups
Large carrot, grated	1	1	1
Can of mandarin oranges in natural juice, drained, reserving the juice	300 g	11 oz	1 medium
Spring onions (scallions), chopped	2	2	2
Piece of cucumber, finely diced	2.5 cm	1 in	1 in
Light soy sauce	30 ml	2 tbsp	2 tbsp
White wine vinegar	15 ml	1 tbsp	1 tbsp
Soya or sunflower oil	15 ml	1 tbsp	1 tbsp

1 Put the soya beans in a salad bowl with the beansprouts, carrot, oranges, spring onions and cucumber.

2 Whisk the remaining ingredients with 30 ml/2 tbsp of the mandarin orange juice. Pour over the salad, toss and chill until ready to serve.

Wild Rice and Prawn Salad

Serves 4

	METRIC	IMPERIAL	AMERICAN
Wild rice mix	175 g	6 oz	¾ cup
Mangetout (snow peas), trimmed	50 g	2 oz	2 oz
Button mushrooms, thinly sliced	50 g	2 oz	2 oz
Cooked peeled prawns (shrimp)	100 g	4 oz	4 oz
Piece of cucumber, finely chopped	2.5 cm	1 in	1 in
Sunflower oil	45 ml	3 tbsp	3 tbsp
White wine vinegar	30 ml	2 tbsp	2 tbsp
A few drops of Tabasco sauce			
Salt and freshly ground black pepper			
Finely chopped parsley	30 ml	2 tbsp	2 tbsp
Chopped thyme	15 ml	1 tbsp	1 tbsp
Thin twists of cucumber, to garnish			

1   Cook the rice according to the packet directions. Add the mangetout for the last 2 minutes of cooking time. Drain, rinse with cold water and drain again.

2   Add the mushrooms, prawns and cucumber and mix in gently.

3   Whisk the oil, vinegar and Tabasco with a little salt and pepper to taste and the herbs. Drizzle over the salad and toss gently. Cover and chill until ready to serve, garnished with thin twists of cucumber.

Thai Fragrant Rice Moulds

Serves 4

	METRIC	IMPERIAL	AMERICAN
Thai fragrant rice, well rinsed	175 g	6 oz	¾ cup
Red (bell) pepper, finely diced	1	1	1
Frozen peas	50 g	2 oz	2 oz
Grated fresh root ginger	5 ml	1 tsp	1 tsp
Chopped coriander (cilantro)	15 ml	1 tbsp	1 tbsp
Sunflower oil	15 ml	1 tbsp	1 tbsp
Lemon juice	10 ml	2 tsp	2 tsp
A pinch of salt			
Freshly ground black pepper			

1   Cook the rice according to the packet directions, adding the red pepper and peas for the last 5 minutes of cooking time. Drain, rinse with cold water and drain again.

2   Add the remaining ingredients and mix thoroughly.

3   Pack into four individual moulds or small cups, pressing down well. Chill.

4   When ready to serve, invert each mould on to a serving plate, hold the mould and the plate, give and good shake and lift off the mould. Repeat with the remaining moulds.

Warm Carrot and Mustard Salad

Serves 4

	METRIC	IMPERIAL	AMERICAN
Large carrots	4–6	4–6	4–6
A little salt and freshly ground black pepper			
Sunflower oil	30 ml	2 tbsp	2 tbsp
Black mustard seeds	30 ml	2 tbsp	2 tbsp
Lemon juice	15 ml	1 tbsp	1 tbsp

1 Thinly pare the carrots in long ribbons with a potato peeler or coarsely grate. Place in a salad bowl. Sprinkle with a little salt and pepper.

2 Heat the oil in a frying pan (skillet) over the coals. Add the mustard seeds. As soon as they start to pop, add the lemon juice, swirl round and pour over the salad. Toss and serve straight away.

Californian Pickled Vegetables

Serves 8

	METRIC	IMPERIAL	AMERICAN
White wine vinegar	300 ml	½ pt	1¼ cups
Water	300 ml	½ pt	1¼ cups
Granulated sugar	225 g	8 oz	1 cup
Pickling spices	15 ml	1 tbsp	1 tbsp
Clove	1	1	1
Small cinnamon stick	1	1	1
Small bay leaf	1	1	1
French (green) beans, topped and tailed	225 g	8 oz	8 oz
Baby sweetcorn (corn) cobs	100 g	4 oz	4 oz
Red (bell) peppers, sliced	2	2	2
Small cauliflower, cut into small florets	½	½	½
Baby carrots, scraped but left whole	100 g	4 oz	4 oz
Button (pearl) onions, peeled but left whole	100 g	4 oz	4 oz
Small cucumber	1	1	1

1   Put the vinegar, water, sugar, pickling spices, clove, cinnamon and bay leaf in a saucepan. Bring slowly to the boil.

2   Meanwhile, put all the vegetables except the cucumber in a pan containing 2.5 cm/1 in boiling water. Cover and cook for 4 minutes. Drain and turn into a large non-metallic bowl.

3 Cut both ends off the cucumber, quarter lengthways and cut into even-sized chunks. Add to the bowl.

4 Pour the boiling vinegar mixture over the vegetables. Cover loosely and leave until cold. Turn into a container with a sealable lid. Cover securely and chill for at least 1 day or up to 3 weeks. Drain thoroughly before serving.

Melon, Cucumber and Tomato Salad

Serves 4

	METRIC	IMPERIAL	AMERICAN
Small honeydew melon, peeled, seeded and cubed	1	1	1
Small cucumber, peeled and diced	1	1	1
Cherry tomatoes, halved	8	8	8
Chopped mint	15 ml	1 tbsp	1 tbsp
Chopped parsley	15 ml	1 tbsp	1 tbsp
Finely grated rind and juice of ½ orange			
Finely grated rind and juice of 1 lemon			
Olive oil	45 ml	3 tbsp	3 tbsp
A pinch of salt			
Freshly ground black pepper			
Bunch of watercress	1	1	1
Toasted pine nuts	15 ml	1 tbsp	1 tbsp

1 Mix the melon with the cucumber and tomatoes in a salad bowl.

2 Whisk all the remaining ingredients except the watercress and pine nuts together and pour over the salad. Toss gently. Chill until ready to serve.

3 Trim the feathery ends of the stalks from the watercress and separate into sprigs. Arrange in a salad bowl. Spoon in the melon mixture and sprinkle with the pine nuts before serving.

Crispy Crunch Salad

Serves 4

	METRIC	IMPERIAL	AMERICAN
Red eating (dessert) apple, unpeeled and diced	1	1	1
Lemon juice	15 ml	1 tbsp	1 tbsp
Small iceburg lettuce, shredded	½	½	½
Bunch of radishes, sliced	1	1	1
Red onion, sliced and separated into rings	1	1	1
Celery sticks, chopped	2	2	2
Olive oil	30 ml	2 tbsp	2 tbsp
Red wine vinegar	15 ml	1 tbsp	1 tbsp
Caster (superfine) sugar	5 ml	1 tsp	1 tsp
Chopped basil	15 ml	1 tbsp	1 tbsp
Salt and freshly ground black pepper			

1 Toss the diced apple in the lemon juice to prevent browning.

2 Put in a salad bowl with the lettuce, radishes, onion and celery.

3 Whisk the oil with the vinegar, sugar, basil and salt and pepper to taste. When ready to serve, pour over the salad, toss and serve.

Spinach, Cucumber and Kiwi Salad

Serves 4

	METRIC	IMPERIAL	AMERICAN
Young spinach leaves, trimmed	100 g	4 oz	4 oz
Kiwi fruit	2	2	2
Cucumber, peeled and thinly sliced	¼	¼	¼
Spring onions (scallions), finely chopped	2	2	2
Olive oil	30 ml	2 tbsp	2 tbsp
White wine vinegar	15 ml	1 tbsp	1 tbsp
Clear honey	5 ml	1 tsp	1 tsp
Chopped thyme	15 ml	1 tbsp	1 tbsp
Chopped parsley	15 ml	1 tbsp	1 tbsp
Salt and freshly ground black pepper			

1 Rinse the spinach thoroughly (it can be gritty) and pat dry on kitchen paper (paper towels). Arrange on a flat serving platter.

2 Peel and halve the kiwi fruit and cut into thin slices.

3 Arrange the cucumber and kiwi slices attractively on the spinach.

4 Whisk the remaining ingredients together and drizzle over. Chill for 30 minutes before serving, to allow the flavours to develop.

BREADS AND OTHER ACCOMPANIMENTS

You can buy plenty of speciality breads but creating your own fresh-baked loaves, savoury rolls or crackers adds a very personal touch to any meal and they are all very simple to make.

Hot Pepper Corn Bread

Makes 8

	METRIC	IMPERIAL	AMERICAN
Self-raising (self-rising) flour	50 g	2 oz	½ cup
Salt	2.5 ml	½ tsp	½ tsp
Baking powder	5 ml	1 tsp	1 tsp
Cornmeal	50 g	2 oz	½ cup
Clear honey	5 ml	1 tsp	1 tsp
Skimmed milk	120 ml	4 fl oz	½ cup
Egg	1	1	1
Jalapeno pepper, seeded and finely chopped	1	1	1
Frozen sweetcorn (corn), thawed	50 g	2 oz	2oz
Monterey Jack or Cheddar cheese, grated	50 g	2 oz	½ cup
Freshly ground black pepper			
Sunflower oil for greasing			

1   Sift the flour, salt and baking powder into a bowl and stir in the cornmeal.

2   Whisk the honey, milk and egg together and stir into the mixture. Add the chilli, corn, cheese and a good grinding of black pepper. Mix well.

3   Grease eight sections of a muffin tin (pan) liberally with oil. Spoon in the corn mixture.

4   Bake in a preheated oven at 230°C/450°F/gas mark 8 for 15 minutes until risen and golden brown. Transfer to a wire rack to cool. Reheat, wrapped in foil, at the side of the barbecue, if liked.

Sesame Rye Thins

Makes about 24

	METRIC	IMPERIAL	AMERICAN
Plain (all-purpose) flour	50 g	2 oz	½ cup
Rye flour	75 g	3 oz	¾ cup
Celery salt	5 ml	1 tsp	1 tsp
Oat bran	50 g	2 oz	½ cup
Sesame seeds	25 g	1 oz	¼ cup
Sunflower oil	45 ml	3 tbsp	3 tbsp
Cold water, to mix	75 ml	5 tbsp	5 tbsp

1   Mix together the flours, celery salt, bran and sesame seeds.

2   Stir in the oil and add enough cold water to form a soft but not sticky dough.

3   Knead gently on a lightly floured surface and roll out thinly. Cut into squares with a knife or biscuit (cookie) cutter.

4   Transfer to a baking (cookie) sheet and bake in a preheated oven at 180°C/350°F/gas mark 4 for about 30 minutes until golden. Transfer to a wire rack to cool. Store in an airtight container.

Sweet Potato Butterhorns

You can use a large drained can of sweet potatoes or yams if you are short of time.

Makes 16

	METRIC	IMPERIAL	AMERICAN
Large sweet potato, peeled and diced	1	1	1
Wholemeal flour	175 g	6 oz	1½ cups
Strong plain (bread) flour	175 g	6 oz	1½ cups
Butter or sunflower spread	25 g	1 oz	2 tbsp
Sachet of easy-blend dried yeast	1	1	1
Light brown sugar	25 g	1 oz	2 tbsp
Large egg, beaten	1	1	1
Hand-hot water	175 ml	6 fl oz	¾ cup
Butter or sunflower spread, to serve			

1 Cook the sweet potato in boiling salted water until tender. Drain well.

2 Turn into a food processor and purée until smooth.

3 Add the flours, butter or spread, yeast and sugar and run the machine until well mixed.

4 Add the egg and, with the machine running, add enough hot water to form a soft but not too sticky dough. Run the machine for a further minute to knead the mixture.

5 Turn the mixture into an oiled plastic bag and leave in a warm place for 1 hour until doubled in bulk.

6   Re-knead the dough, then divide into eight equal pieces. Roll each piece into an 15 cm/5 in square. Cut in half to form triangles. Dampen with a little water.

7   Starting at the long edge, roll up each triangle, then curve the points round to form crescents. Transfer to a greased baking (cookie) sheet.

8   Cover with greased clingfilm (plastic wrap) and leave in a warm place for about 20 minutes to rise. Remove the clingfilm and bake in a preheated oven at 230°C/450°F/gas mark 8 for about 15 minutes until risen and golden and the bases sound hollow when tapped. Serve warm with butter or sunflower spread.

Crisp Fried Tortillas

These are a great accompaniment to Mexican-style food.

Makes 6

	METRIC	IMPERIAL	AMERICAN
Flour tortillas	6	6	6
Oil for deep-frying			

1   Separate the tortillas.

2   Heat the oil until a cube of day-old bread browns in 30 seconds. Deep-fry the tortillas, one at a time, gently submerging them in the oil with a fish slice, until crisp and golden, about 2 minutes. Drain on kitchen paper (paper towels). Serve in a stack.

Crunchy Pecan Rolls

You can buy brown bread mix with sunflower seeds included. If you use this, omit the sunflower seeds in the recipe.

Makes 8

	METRIC	IMPERIAL	AMERICAN
Packet of wholemeal bread mix	283 g	10¼ oz	10¼ oz
Butter or sunflower spread	25 g	1 oz	2 tbsp
Pecan nuts, roughly chopped	50 g	2 oz	½ cup
Sunflower seeds	15 ml	1 tbsp	1 tbsp
Hand-hot water	175 ml	6 fl oz	¾ cup
Low-fat soft cheese, to serve			

1 Empty the bread mix into a bowl and rub in the butter or spread.

2 Stir in the nuts and seeds and mix with the water to form a firm dough.

3 Knead gently on a lightly floured surface for 5 minutes.

4 Divide into eight pieces and shape into balls. Place well apart on a greased baking (cookie) sheet. Cover loosely with greased clingfilm (plastic wrap) and leave in a warm place for about 45 minutes until doubled in bulk.

5 Remove the clingfilm and bake in a preheated oven at 200°C/400°F/gas mark 6 for about 10–12 minutes until golden and the bases sound hollow when tapped. Cool on a wire rack.

6 Wrap in foil and warm at the side of the barbecue. Serve split with soft cheese for spreading.

Ciabatta with Onions and Sun-dried Tomatoes

Serves 6

	METRIC	IMPERIAL	AMERICAN
Ciabatta loaf	1	1	1
Butter or sunflower spread	75 g	3 oz	⅓ cup
Large onion, finely chopped	1	1	1
Sun-dried tomatoes in oil, drained and finely chopped	4	4	4
Chopped parsley	30 ml	2 tbsp	2 tbsp
Freshly ground black pepper			
Olive oil	30 ml	2 tbsp	2 tbsp

1 Cut the loaf in half horizontally, not right through, so that the top and bottom are still attached.

2 Heat half the butter or sunflower spread in a frying pan (skillet) and fry (sauté) the onion for 2 minutes to soften.

3 Stir in the remaining butter or spread with the tomatoes, parsley and a good grinding of pepper and mix well. Spread this mixture into the cut loaf. Re-shape, brush with the oil and wrap in foil, shiny side in.

4 Cook on the barbecue for about 15 minutes, turning frequently, until the crust feels crisp when squeezed. Serve cut into slices.

Garlic and Herb Baguette

Serves 4–6

	METRIC	IMPERIAL	AMERICAN
Small French stick	1	1	1
Butter or sunflower spread	75 g	3 oz	⅓ cup
Garlic cloves, crushed	1–2	1–2	1–2
Chopped parsley	15 ml	1 tbsp	1 tbsp
Chopped sage	10 ml	2 tsp	2 tsp
Chopped oregano	10 ml	2 tsp	2 tsp

1 Cut the French stick into 12 slices, not right through the base crust.

2 Mash the butter or spread with the garlic and herbs and spread between each slice, spreading any remainder over the top crust.

3 Wrap in foil, shiny side in. Cook on the barbecue for about 15 minutes, turning frequently until the crust feels crisp when squeezed. Unwrap and serve.

Focaccia-style Pitta Pockets

Serves 4

	METRIC	IMPERIAL	AMERICAN
Olive oil	45 ml	3 tbsp	3 tbsp
Spanish onions, thinly sliced	3	3	3
Large garlic cloves, crushed	2	2	2
Chopped oregano	15 ml	1 tbsp	1 tbsp
Salt and freshly ground black pepper			
Pitta breads	4	4	4

1 Heat all but 10 ml/2 tsp of the oil and fry (sauté) the onions gently until softened but not browned. Add the garlic and oregano and season with salt and pepper.

2 Cut the pitta breads in half widthways and gently open along the cuts to form pockets.

3 Spoon the onion mixture inside. Brush all over with oil and wrap in foil, shiny side in.

4 Place on the barbecue for 2–3 minutes on each side until hot through. Unwrap and serve.

Over-the-coals Damper

Serves 4

	METRIC	IMPERIAL	AMERICAN
Self-raising (self-rising) flour	350 g	12 oz	3 cups
Salt	5 ml	1 tsp	1 tsp
Dried milk powder (non-fat dry milk)	15 ml	1 tbsp	1 tbsp
Butter or sunflower spread	25 g	1 oz	2 tbsp
Water	300 ml	½ pt	1¼ cups

1 Mix the flour and salt with the dried milk.

2 Rub in the butter or spread.

3 Mix in the water with a knife to form a dough. Knead in the bowl until smooth.

4 Shape into a round, flatten and place on a piece of floured foil, shiny side up.

5 Make a few slashes in the top with a knife and wrap securely in the foil. Put directly on the hot coals and cook for about 15–20 minutes, turning once, until golden brown and the base sounds hollow when tapped. Serve hot, broken into pieces.

DRESSINGS, SAUCES AND RELISHES

The most ordinary green salad can be transformed by tossing it in a light, fragrant dressing. A freshly prepared relish will add zip and colour to the plainest steak and just adding a sweet sauce to a barbecued banana will make a magical dessert. Choose any of these to brighten up even the simplest barbecue fare.

~~~~~~~~~~~~~~

Light French Dressing

Serves 4–6

	METRIC	IMPERIAL	AMERICAN
Olive oil	30 ml	2 tbsp	2 tbsp
White wine vinegar	30 ml	2 tbsp	2 tbsp
Water	30 ml	2 tbsp	2 tbsp
Dijon mustard	5 ml	1 tsp	1 tsp
Chopped parsley	15 ml	1 tbsp	1 tbsp
Chopped oregano	15 ml	1 tbsp	1 tbsp
A pinch of caster (superfine) sugar			
Salt and freshly ground black pepper			

Whisk all the ingredients together and use as required.

Creamy Garlic Dressing

Serves 4–6

	METRIC	IMPERIAL	AMERICAN
Olive oil	15 ml	1 tbsp	1 tbsp
Low-fat crème fraîche	75 ml	5 tbsp	5 tbsp
Lemon juice	30 ml	2 tbsp	2 tbsp
Garlic clove, crushed	1	1	1
Chopped parsley	15 ml	1 tbsp	1 tbsp
Salt and freshly ground black pepper			
Clear honey	5 ml	1 tsp	1 tsp
A little cold milk			

Whisk all the ingredients together, adding enough milk to thin to a pouring consistency. Chill until ready to serve.

Sun-dried Tomato Vinaigrette

Serves 4

	METRIC	IMPERIAL	AMERICAN
Sun-dried tomatoes in oil	3	3	3
Sun-dried tomato oil	30 ml	2 tbsp	2 tbsp
Sunflower oil	15 ml	1 tbsp	1 tbsp
Red wine vinegar	30 ml	2 tbsp	2 tbsp
Apple juice	15 ml	1 tbsp	1 tbsp
Salt and freshly ground black pepper			

Put all the ingredients in a blender or food processor. Run the machine until smooth. Thin with a little extra apple juice, if necessary. Use as required.

Pine Nut Dressing

Serves 6

	METRIC	IMPERIAL	AMERICAN
Pine nuts, toasted	100 g	4 oz	⅔ cup
Olive oil	90 ml	6 tbsp	6 tbsp
Lemon juice	30 ml	2 tbsp	2 tbsp
Chopped tarragon	15 ml	1 tbsp	1 tbsp
A good pinch of ground cinnamon			
Clear honey	10 ml	2 tsp	2 tsp
Salt and freshly ground black pepper			

Put all the ingredients in a screw-topped jar and shake vigorously until well blended. Chill overnight.

Soured Cream and Chive Topping

This and the following three toppings are delicious with jacket potatoes; spoon over before serving or hand them separately.

Serves 4

	METRIC	IMPERIAL	AMERICAN
Soured (dairy sour) cream	150 ml	¼ pt	⅔ cup
Snipped chives	30 ml	2 tbsp	2 tbsp
Dried onion granules	2.5 ml	½ tsp	½ tsp
A pinch of salt			
Freshly ground black pepper			

Mix all the ingredients together in a small bowl and chill until ready to serve.

Prawn Topping

Serves 4

	METRIC	IMPERIAL	AMERICAN
Low-calorie mayonnaise	75 ml	5 tbsp	5 tbsp
Plain low-fat yoghurt	75 ml	5 tbsp	5 tbsp
Tomato ketchup (catsup)	15 ml	1 tbsp	1 tbsp
Lemon juice	5 ml	1 tsp	1 tsp
Worcestershire sauce	5 ml	1 tsp	1 tsp
A few drops of Tabasco sauce			
Freshly ground black pepper			
Small cooked prawns (shrimp), peeled	100 g	4 oz	4 oz

1 Mix all the ingredients except the prawns together until well blended.

2 Dry the prawns on kitchen paper (paper towels), if previously frozen.

3 Fold into the sauce and chill until ready to serve.

Garlic and Herb Cheese and Tomato Topping

Serves 4

	METRIC	IMPERIAL	AMERICAN
Garlic and herb soft cheese	100g	4 oz	½ cup
Milk	75 ml	5 tbsp	5 tbsp
Large tomato, skinned, seeded and finely chopped	1	1	1
Finely chopped parsley	15 ml	1 tbsp	1 tbsp
Freshly ground black pepper			

1 Put the cheese in a bowl and gradually work in enough of the milk to form a smooth thick sauce.

2 Stir in the tomato and parsley and season with pepper. Chill until ready to serve.

Herby Mushroom Yoghurt Topping

Serves 4

	METRIC	IMPERIAL	AMERICAN
Button mushrooms, finely chopped	75 g	3 oz	3 oz
Onion, finely chopped	1	1	1
Butter or sunflower spread	15 g	½ oz	1 tbsp
Dried marjoram	2.5 ml	½ tsp	½ tsp
Low-fat plain yoghurt	120 ml	4 fl oz	½ cup
Snipped chives	15 ml	1 tbsp	1 tbsp
Salt and freshly ground black pepper			

1 Cook the mushrooms and onions very gently in the butter or spread for 2 minutes.

2 Add the marjoram, cover and cook over a gentle heat for 5 minutes, stirring occasionally, until soft and juicy. Remove from the heat, turn into a small bowl and leave to cool.

3 Stir in the yoghurt, chives and seasoning to taste. Chill until ready to serve.

Barbecue Sauce

Serves 4–6

	METRIC	IMPERIAL	AMERICAN
Garlic clove, crushed	1	1	1
Small onion, very finely chopped	1	1	1
Sunflower oil	10 ml	2 tsp	2 tsp
Tomato purée (paste)	100 g	4 oz	4 oz
Fruity dry white wine	300 ml	½ pt	1¼ cups
Light soy sauce	10 ml	2 tsp	2 tsp
Clear honey	30 ml	2 tbsp	2 tbsp
White wine vinegar	30 ml	2 tbsp	2 tbsp
A few drops of Tabasco sauce			
Salt and freshly ground black pepper			

1   Put the garlic, onion and oil in a small saucepan suitable for transferring to the barbecue. Cook for 2 minutes, stirring, until the onion is softened.

2   Add the remaining ingredients, bring to the boil, reduce the heat and simmer for about 20 minutes until thick. Taste and re-season, if necessary.

3   Keep warm at the side of the barbecue. Serve with any barbecued meats, fish or vegetables.

Orange and Mango Salsa

Serves 4–6

	METRIC	IMPERIAL	AMERICAN
Large just-ripe mango	1	1	1
Spring onions (scallions), finely chopped	4–6	4–6	4–6
Oranges	2	2	2
Small red chilli, seeded and chopped	1	1	1
Chopped mint	15 ml	1 tbsp	1 tbsp
Grated fresh root ginger	2.5 ml	½ tsp	½ tsp
A pinch of salt			
Freshly ground black pepper			
Lemon juice	5 ml	1 tsp	1 tsp

1   Peel the mango and cut all the fruit off the stone (pit). Cut into small dice and place in a bowl.

2   Add the spring onions.

3   Finely grate the rind from one of the oranges. Cut off all the peel and pith from both. Slice the fruit, then cut into small pieces. Add to the mango and onion.

4   Add the remaining ingredients and mix well. Cover and chill for at least 1 hour to allow the flavours to develop. Serve with barbecued fish or chicken.

Guacamole Relish

Serves 6

	METRIC	IMPERIAL	AMERICAN
Large ripe avocados	2	2	2
Lemon juice	15 ml	1 tbsp	1 tbsp
Shallot, grated	1	1	1
Sunflower oil	90 ml	6 tbsp	6 tbsp
Worcestershire sauce	15 ml	1 tbsp	1 tbsp
A few drops of Tabasco sauce			
Tomatoes, seeded and finely chopped	2	2	2
Piece of cucumber, finely chopped	2.5 cm	1 in	1 in

1 Halve the avocados, remove the stones (pits) and scoop the flesh out of the skins into a bowl.

2 Mash well with a fork, then mash in the lemon juice and shallot.

3 Gradually beat in the oil, a few drops at a time, until thick and fairly smooth (if the mixture curdles, gradually beat it into 15 ml/1 tbsp mayonnaise).

4 Flavour with the Worcestershire sauce and Tabasco to taste. Fold in the chopped tomato and cucumber just before serving.

Caviar Cream

Serves 4–6

	METRIC	IMPERIAL	AMERICAN
Low-fat crème fraîche	150 ml	¼ pt	⅔ cup
Finely grated lemon rind	5 ml	1 tsp	1 tsp
Chopped dill (dill weed)	15 ml	1 tbsp	1 tbsp
Jar of Danish lumpfish roe	50 g	2 oz	1 small
Freshly ground black pepper			

1 Put the crème fraîche, lemon rind and dill in a small bowl and chill. Chill the jar of lumpfish roe separately.

2 Just before serving, fold in the lumpfish roe and season with pepper. Serve with all types of seafood.

Amaretto Cream

Serves 4–6

	METRIC	IMPERIAL	AMERICAN
Double (heavy) cream	150 ml	¼ pt	⅔ cup
Caster (superfine) sugar	30 ml	2 tbsp	2 tbsp
Amaretto liqueur	30 ml	2 tbsp	2 tbsp
Toasted chopped almonds, to decorate	15 ml	1 tbsp	1 tbsp

1 Empty the cream into a bowl and whip until beginning to thicken.

2 Add the sugar and liqueur and whip gently until softly peaking. Turn into a small bowl, sprinkle with the almonds and chill until ready to serve.

Chilled Lemon Sauce

Serves 6

	METRIC	IMPERIAL	AMERICAN
Lemon curd	90 ml	6 tbsp	6 tbsp
Low-fat crème fraîche	45 ml	3 tbsp	3 tbsp
Lemon juice	15 ml	1 tbsp	1 tbsp
Milk			

Mix all the ingredients together, adding enough milk to form a thick pouring consistency. Turn into a small jug and chill until required.

DESSERTS

Unless you have a gas barbecue that you can turn on and off at a moment's notice, you will probably find you have much more heat than you need to cook just one or two courses. So round off your barbecue with a simple but delicious dessert that can cook over the coals while you finish your main course. Alternatively, let your guests have a bit of a rest while you barbecue the perfect end to the meal.

~~~~~~~~~~~~~~~

Chocolate Apricot French Toasts

Serves 4

	METRIC	IMPERIAL	AMERICAN
Slices of white bread, crusts removed	8	8	8
Butter or sunflower spread	25 g	1 oz	2 tbsp
Apricot jam (conserve)	60 ml	4 tbsp	4 tbsp
Plain (semi-sweet) chocolate, grated	100 g	4 oz	1 cup
Ground cinnamon	1.5 ml	¼ tsp	¼ tsp
Icing (confectioners') sugar, to decorate	30 ml	2 tbsp	2 tbsp

1 Spread the bread thinly with butter or sunflower spread on one side.

2 Put four slices, buttered side down, on squares of foil, shiny sides up.

3 Spread with the jam and sprinkle with the chocolate. Dust with the cinnamon.

4 Cover with the remaining slices of bread, buttered sides out. Wrap loosely, but securely in foil.

5 Barbecue for about 4 minutes on each side until the bread is toasted and the chocolate has melted.

6 Unwrap on plates, cut into triangles and dust with sifted icing sugar before serving.

Strawberry, Apricot and Spice-cube Kebabs

Serves 6

	METRIC	IMPERIAL	AMERICAN
Thick slices of white bread, crusts removed	2	2	2
Butter or sunflower spread, melted	40 g	1½ oz	3 tbsp
Mixed (apple-pie) spice	5 ml	1 tsp	1 tsp
Caster (superfine) sugar	30 ml	2 tbsp	2 tbsp
Large ripe strawberries	12	12	12
Apricots, halved and stoned (pitted)	6	6	6
Chilled Lemon Sauce (see page 136), to serve			

1 Cut each slice of the bread into nine cubes. Place in a dish and toss in 25 g/1 oz/2 tbsp of the melted butter or spread.

2 Mix the spice and sugar together, add the bread and toss to coat.

3 Thread the bread and fruit alternately on six soaked wooden skewers.

4 Barbecue for 5 minutes, turning once or twice and brushing with the remaining melted butter or spread, until the bread is golden and the fruit hot. Serve straight away with Chilled Lemon Sauce.

Butter Nut Sweet Potatoes

Serves 6

	METRIC	IMPERIAL	AMERICAN
Sweet potatoes, about 175 g/6 oz each, scrubbed	3	3	3
Butter or sunflower spread, melted	75 g	3 oz	⅓ cup
Fresh dates, stoned (pitted) and chopped	6	6	6
Maple syrup	45 ml	3 tbsp	3 tbsp
Pecans, chopped	50 g	2 oz	½ cup
Lemon juice	10 ml	2 tsp	2 tsp
Vanilla ice cream, to serve			

1 Boil the sweet potatoes in water for about 15–20 minutes until they feel just tender. Drain, rinse with cold water and drain again.

2 Peel and cut into halves lengthways.

3 Scoop out the centre of each potato with a small spoon or a melon baller, leaving a thick shell. Chop the scooped-out flesh.

4 Brush six squares of foil, shiny sides up, with a little of the butter or spread. Stand a scooped-out sweet potato half on each one.

5 Mix the chopped sweet potato with the dates, syrup, half the remaining butter or spread, the nuts and lemon juice and spoon into the sweet potato shells. Brush with the remaining butter.

6 Wrap in the foil and barbecue for about 5 minutes until piping hot. Open, transfer to serving plates and serve with a scoop of ice cream on top.

West Coast Pears

Serves 4

	METRIC	IMPERIAL	AMERICAN
Ripe dessert pears	4	4	4
Californian raisins	25 g	1 oz	⅙ cup
Almond paste, grated	50 g	2 oz	2 oz
Sunflower oil	15 ml	1 tbsp	1 tbsp
Caster (superfine) sugar	15 ml	1 tbsp	1 tbsp
Amaretto Cream (see page 135), to serve			

1 Cut the pears into halves but do not peel. Cut out the cores to leave small cavities.

2 Mix the raisins with the almond paste. Sandwich the pear halves back together with this mixture.

3 Brush with oil, dust with sugar and wrap firmly in foil, shiny sides in.

4 Cook on the barbecue for about 10–15 minutes, turning occasionally, until hot through. Unwrap and serve with Amaretto Cream.

Poached Peaches in Chardonnay

Serves 4

	METRIC	IMPERIAL	AMERICAN
Large ripe peaches	4	4	4
Californian Chardonnay	300 ml	½ pt	1¼ cups
Water	150 ml	¼ pt	⅔ cup
Light brown sugar	30 ml	2 tbsp	2 tbsp
Piece of cinnamon stick	1	1	1
Vanilla ice cream, to serve			

1 Plunge the peaches into boiling water for 30 seconds. Drain and peel off the skins.

2 Put the remaining ingredients in a saucepan suitable for placing on the barbecue, and stir until the sugar has dissolved. Add the fruit and cover with a lid.

3 Transfer to the barbecue and poach for about 8–10 minutes.

4 Serve hot with vanilla ice cream.

Frosted Grapes with Grilled Brie

You can frost the grapes by simply dipping them in water and then dusting with sugar but the effect is not so professional.

Serves 4

	METRIC	IMPERIAL	AMERICAN
Small bunches of red seedless grapes	4	4	4
Small bunches of green seedless grapes	4	4	4
Egg white, lightly beaten	1	1	1
Caster (superfine) sugar for sprinkling			
Wedges of Brie, each about 75 g/3 oz	4	4	4
Digestive biscuits (Graham crackers), to serve			

1   Brush the bunches of grapes all over with the egg white, then sprinkle liberally with the sugar. Lay on a sheet of greaseproof (waxed) paper and leave to dry.

2   When ready to serve, arrange one red and one green bunch of grapes on each of four serving plates.

3   Lay the cheese on a sheet of foil and cook on the barbecue until the cheese begins to melt. Quickly transfer to the serving plates and serve straight away with digestive biscuits.

Blueberry and Mallow Surprises

Serves 4

	METRIC	IMPERIAL	AMERICAN
A little butter or sunflower spread for greasing			
Eating (dessert) apples, peeled, cored and cut into rings	2	2	2
Finely grated rind and juice of ½ lemon			
Blueberries	100 g	4 oz	4 oz
Marshmallows	100 g	4 oz	4 oz
Fromage frais, to serve			

1 Lightly grease four squares of foil, shiny side up.

2 Lay apple slices in the middle of each piece and sprinkle with the lemon rind and juice. Scatter the blueberries over.

3 Snip the marshmallows with wet scissors and scatter over. Wrap loosely but securely in the foil.

4 Barbecue for about 8–10 minutes until the apple feels just tender and the marshmallows have melted. Transfer the parcels to serving plates, open at the table and eat out of the foil with fromage frais.

Quick-cook Bananas with Coffee Liqueur

Serves 4

	METRIC	IMPERIAL	AMERICAN
Ripe bananas, unpeeled	4	4	4
Coffee liqueur	60 ml	4 tbsp	4 tbsp
Scoops of coffee ice cream, to serve	4	4	4

1 Lay the bananas on the barbecue and cook, turning once or twice, until the bananas are blackened on the outside and feel soft.

2 Split along one edge and carefully open. Pour the coffee liqueur into the split and serve with a scoop of coffee ice cream on the side. Eat out of the skins with a spoon.

Honeyed Figs and Dates with Pine Nuts

Serves 4

	METRIC	IMPERIAL	AMERICAN
A little butter or sunflower spread for greasing			
Fresh ripe figs, halved	4	4	4
Fresh dates, halved and stoned (pitted)	8	8	8
Clear blossom or heather honey	60 ml	4 tbsp	4 tbsp
Pine nuts, chopped	25 g	1 oz	¼ cup
Small lime, quartered	1	1	1
Greek-style yoghurt	150 ml	¼ pt	⅔ cup

1 Grease four squares of foil, shiny sides up.

2 Lay two halves of fig on each sheet and arrange the halved dates around.

3 Drizzle with the honey. Sprinkle with the nuts and squeeze a lime quarter over each.

4 Wrap loosely but securely in the foil. Cook on the barbecue for 8–10 minutes until the figs are tender.

5 Transfer the parcels to serving plates. Open at the table and serve with Greek-style yoghurt.

Star Pain au Chocolat

Serves 4

	METRIC	IMPERIAL	AMERICAN
Butter or sunflower spread, melted	25 g	1 oz	2 tbsp
Star fruit, sliced	4	4	4
Caster (superfine) sugar	20 ml	4 tsp	4 tsp
Mini pains au chocolat	4	4	4
Bottled chocolate sauce for ice cream			

1 Brush a sheet of foil with a little of the butter or spread. Place on the barbecue.

2 Lay the star fruit slices on the foil in a single layer and brush with the remaining butter or spread. Sprinkle with half the sugar, turn over and sprinkle again.

3 Barbecue for 2 minutes on each side. Add the pains au chocolat and cook for about 1 minute until they are crisp and the star fruit are turning golden at the edges.

4 Arrange a circle of star fruit slices on each of four serving plates. Put a pain au chocolat in the centre of each. Drizzle the fruit with a little chocolate sauce and serve straight away.

REFRESHING DRINKS

Although the food is obviously the main part of a
barbecue, the drink is very important too. Californian
wines are amongst some of the finest in the world and
are readily available. Serve white or rosé wine well
chilled. Most reds, except very young wines, are best
served at room (or garden!) temperature. Some people
prefer to serve chilled lager or cider with the meal.
These are not so typically Californian, but there are
many varieties to choose from. Do make sure they are
very cold – warm beer is a complete disaster!
But if you really want to make the party go with a
swing, why not serve a delicious fruit cup or cocktail to
kick off the event? Here is a thirst-quenching selection
of both alcoholic and non-alcoholic drinks for you to
try. Don't forget to have plenty of chilled mineral water
too, especially when the weather is at its hottest.

~~~~~~~~~~~~~~

The Freshest Lemonade

Serves 8

	METRIC	IMPERIAL	AMERICAN
Large lemons, well washed	6	6	6
Granulated sugar	225 g	8 oz	1 cup
Water	1.5 litres	2½ pts	6 cups
A good pinch of grated nutmeg			
Ice cubes			
Sprigs of mint, to garnish			

1   Halve the lemons and squeeze out all the juice into a large pan. Add the lemon shells and the sugar.

2   Add half the water and heat gently, stirring, until the sugar has completely dissolved. Bring to the boil. Remove from the heat, stir in the remaining water and nutmeg and leave until cold. Strain into a large jug, then chill.

3   Pour into tall glasses over ice cubes and garnish with sprigs of mint.

Iced Tea Cup

You can cheat and use instant lemon tea. As this is often already sweetened, you may not need the sugar, so taste first!

Serves 10

	METRIC	IMPERIAL	AMERICAN
Strong black tea, made with 2 tea bags	300 ml	½ pt	1¼ cups
Water	1 litre	1¾ pts	4¼ cups
Granulated sugar	225 g	8 oz	1 cup
Lemon juice	90 ml	6 tbsp	6 tbsp
Pure orange juice	300 ml	½ pt	1¼ cups
Pure apple juice	300 ml	½ pt	1¼ cups
Pure pineapple juice	300 ml	½ pt	1¼ cups
Club soda or sparkling lemonade, chilled	1 litre	1¾ pts	4¼ cups

1 Mix everything exept the soda or lemonade in a large container. Chill thoroughly.

2 Add the soda or lemonade just before serving.

Mint Julep

Serves 6

	METRIC	IMPERIAL	AMERICAN
Chopped mint	30 ml	2 tbsp	2 tbsp
Granulated sugar	100 g	4 oz	½ cup
Juice of 2 lemons			
Juice of 2 oranges			
Water	300 ml	½ pt	1¼ cups
American ginger ale	1 litre	1¾ pts	4¼ cups
Crushed ice			
Fresh mint leaves			

1 Mix the chopped mint, sugar, lemon and orange juice and water together. Stir until the sugar has dissolved, then chill for at least 2 hours.

2 Strain into a large jug and add the ginger ale just before serving.

3 Pour over crushed ice in tall glasses and garnish with a few mint leaves.

Sparkling Peach and Apple Cocktail

Serves 8

	METRIC	IMPERIAL	AMERICAN
Ripe peaches, skinned, stoned (pitted) and roughly chopped	4	4	4
Juice of 1 lime			
Apple juice	250 ml	8 fl oz	1 cup
Grated fresh root ginger	2.5 ml	½ tsp	½ tsp
American ginger ale	1.2 litres	2 pts	5 cups
Crushed ice			
Lime slices, to garnish			

1 Purée the peaches in a blender or food processor with the lime juice.

2 Blend in the apple juice and ginger.

3 Pour into a jug and chill until ready to serve.

4 Stir in the ginger ale, pour over crushed ice in tall glasses and serve, garnished with a lime slice on the rim of each glass.

Orchard Spritzers

Serves 6

	METRIC	IMPERIAL	AMERICAN
Dry sherry	300 ml	½ pt	1¼ cups
Medium cider	450 ml	¾ pt	2 cups
Ice cubes			
Club soda			

1 Mix the sherry and cider together and pour into tall glasses over ice.

2 Top up with club soda and serve immediately.

Cran-apple Sling

Serves 6–8

	METRIC	IMPERIAL	AMERICAN
Medium cider	1 litre	1¾ pts	4¼ cups
Cranberry juice drink	1 litre	1¾ pts	4¼ cups
Vodka	150 ml	¼ pt	⅔ cup
Lemonade or lemon soda	600 ml	1 pt	2½ cups
Ice			
Lemon slices, to garnish			

1 Mix the cider with the cranberry juice drink and vodka. Chill.

2 Just before serving, add the lemonade or lemon soda and pour into tall glasses over ice. Hang a slice of lemon on the rim of each glass.

All-day Tequila Cocktail

Serves 6–8

	METRIC	IMPERIAL	AMERICAN
Tequila	300 ml	½ pt	1¼ cups
Caster (superfine) sugar	50 g	2 oz	¼ cup
Juice of 4 limes			
Pineapple juice	300 ml	½ pt	1¼ cups
Crushed ice			
Sparkling mineral water	1 litre	1¾ pts	4¼ cups

1 Mix the tequila with the sugar, lime juice and pineapple juice in a large jug, stirring until the sugar has dissolved. Chill until ready to serve.

2 Pour over crushed ice in tall tumblers and top with sparkling mineral water. Stir and serve.

Mango Refresher

Serves 6

	METRIC	IMPERIAL	AMERICAN
Large ripe mangos	2	2	2
Apple juice	300 ml	½ pt	1¼ cups
Lime juice	30 ml	2 tbsp	2 tbsp
Orange liqueur	30 ml	2 tbsp	2 tbsp
Bottle of dry white wine	1	1	1
Sparkling lemonade			

1 Peel the mangos and cut all the flesh off the stones (pits). Purée in a blender or food processor with the apple and lime juices.

2 Pour into a jug and stir in the orange liqueur and wine. Chill until ready to serve.

3 Top up with sparkling lemonade to taste and serve in tall glasses.

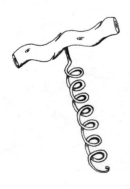

Sangria

Serves 6–8

	METRIC	IMPERIAL	AMERICAN
Ice cubes			
Orange, sliced	1	1	1
Lemon, sliced	1	1	1
Brandy	45 ml	3 tbsp	3 tbsp
Bottle of full-bodied red wine	1	1	1
Lemonade	150 ml	¼ pt	⅔ cup

Half-fill a large jug with ice. Add all the remaining ingredients, stir well and serve.

Planters' Punch

Serves 6–8

	METRIC	IMPERIAL	AMERICAN
Dark rum	300 ml	½ pt	1¼ cups
Grenadine syrup	90 ml	6 tbsp	6 tbsp
Pure orange juice	450 ml	¾ pt	2 cups
Pure pineapple juice	450 ml	¾ pt	2 cups
Lime, thinly sliced	1	1	1
Ice cubes			

1 Mix all the ingredients except the ice in a tall jug. Chill until ready to serve.

2 Pour over ice cubes in tall glasses and serve.

INDEX